iDentities

PAUL SELIGSON
LUIZ OTÁVIO BARROS with **DEBORAH GOLDBLATT**
and **DAMIAN WILLIAMS**

STUDENT'S BOOK & WORKBOOK
2B
COMBO EDITION

Language Map – Student's Book

	Speaking / Topic	Grammar	Vocabulary / Strategies	Writing
7				
7.1	What are our most important years?		Expressions for describing milestones (*come of age, make it through,* etc.)	
7.2	Would you like to live to be 100?	Future perfect vs. future continuous	Expressions for clarifying opinions (*What I mean is that …, What I was trying to say is that …,* etc.)	
7.3	Do babies ever surprise you? (Authentic reading: article on surprising things babies can do)		Adjective-noun collocations in writing and speech	
7.4	Do you seem younger or older than you are?	Cleft sentences: subject and object (e.g. *It's my grandmother who can walk three miles.*)		
7.5	What would your ideal job be?		Expressions for making formal requests	An application letter: more formal alternatives to cleft sentences (*Working in a hotel is rewarding,* etc.)
8				
8.1	What makes a restaurant special?		Expressions with *take* for discussing events; Describing negative experiences	
8.2	Are you a demanding customer?	Subjunctive: verbs and expressions (*I insist that …, it's important that …* etc.)		
8.3	What are the worst aspects of air travel? (Authentic reading: article about amazing customer service)		Expressions of help (*took it upon himself to, went to great lengths to,* etc.)	
8.4	Have you ever borrowed money?	Information focus: adverb clauses to emphasize conditions or contrasts (*As useful as the manual may be, it didn't help; However reasonable the price may seem, its too high,* etc.)	Money terms (*borrow, loan, profit, inherit, tax,* etc.)	
8.5	What was the last complaint you made?			A formal complaint letter (formulas: *to no avail, to resolve the matter,* etc.; passive expressions: *It was my understanding that …, I was led to believe that …,* etc.)
Review 4 p.92				
9				
9.1	Would you like to be a teacher?		"Out-verbs" (*outsmart, outnumber,* etc.); Drawing tentative conclusions	
9.2	What is alternative medicine?	Passive expressions with active and passive infinitives (*The treatment is thought to work well, Patients are known to have been helped,* etc.)	Three-word phrasal verbs (*come down with, give up on,* etc.)	
9.3	What unconventional families do you know? (Authentic reading: article about single parenting)		Common collocations and compounds (*fictitious belief, fairytale ending,* etc.)	
9.4	How often do you work out?	Overview of verb patterns: with base forms, infinitives, and -ing forms	Fitness words (*treadmill, stretching,* etc.); Verbs ending in -en (*whiten, lengthen,* etc.)	
9.5	What are the pros and cons of dieting?		Reacting to new information (*I should reserve judgment, Did I hear you correctly?,* etc.)	A report on pros and cons: using consistent style in lists
10				
10.1	Why do friends drift apart?		Expressions with *say* and *tell* (*it goes without saying, truth be told,* etc.); Friendship idioms (*the life of the party, a breath of fresh air,* etc.)	
10.2	Who's the oldest person you know?	Degrees of comparison with *the … the, more / … er,* and *as … as* (*the more friends you have, the happier you'll feel, friends are nowhere near as important as family,* etc.)		
10.3	How easy is it to make friends where you live? (Authentic reading: the nature of American friendship)		Words with both prefixes and suffixes (double affixation) (*dis-, il-, iln-, ir-, un-* + root + *-able, -al, -ful, -ible, -ive -ity*)	
10.4	Have you ever met someone new by chance?	Inverted conditional sentences for present, past, or future time (*Had she not gone to the party, we wouldn't be married today,* etc.)	Expressions with odds (*What are the odds that …?,* etc.)	
10.5	How persuasive are you?			A persuasive opinion essay: logically building an argument (review of topic sentences; words appealing to common sense, conjunctions, and time markers)
Review 5 p.114				

Language Map – Student's Book

	Speaking / Topic	Grammar	Vocabulary / Strategies	Writing
11				
11.1	What was the last risk you took?		Risk-taking expressions (*play it safe, err on the side of caution*, etc.); Expressing hesitation and encouragement (*There's just too much at stake, What do you have to lose?*, etc.)	
11.2	Do you enjoy riding a bike?	Special uses of modals (expectation, suggestion, refusal, annoyance)	Expressing danger and fear (*He froze in his tracks, He screeched to a halt*, etc.)	
11.3	Are you in favor of online dating? (Authentic reading: article on online dating safety)		Strategies for whether to look up words (guessing words in context, deciding whether they're for active use, etc.)	
11.4	What does the sea make you think of?	Definite and indefinite articles: general and specific use (countable and non-count nouns, first mention, adjective + number, shared knowledge, adjective for a group)		
11.5	Have you ever had an allergic reaction?		Talking about symptoms (*itching, swelling*, etc.)	A statistical report: subject-verb agreement (fractions, percentages, *half, one, a number, the number*, etc.)
12				
12.1	What brands are the wave of the future?		Verbs describing trends (*skyrocket, plummet*, etc.); Expressing cause and reason (*stem from, is closely related to*, etc.)	
12.2	What songs have changed the world?	Passive forms with gerunds and infinitives (*I remember being told about it; New facts seem to be discovered all the time*, etc.)	Transitive and intransitive phrasal verbs	
12.3	What futuristic programs have you seen? (Authentic reading: predicting the future 100 years ago)		Looking up words	
12.4	How unpredictable has your life been?	The passive with *get* and *be*; the causative with *get* and *have* (*get* passive to express informality, emphasis, negative intent, and unintended consequences)	Expressions with *worth* (*worth the effort, worth my time*, etc.)	
12.5	What will make a better society?		*Whatsoever* to emphasize negative ideas	An opinion essay: using verb phrases and noun phrases to avoid repetition

Review 6 *p.136*

Grammar expansion *p.150*

Workbook contents

Unit 7 .... Page 33
Unit 8 .... Page 38
Unit 9 .... Page 43
Unit 10 .... Page 48
Unit 11 .... Page 53
Unit 12 .... Page 58
Selected audio scripts .... Page 65
Answer key .... Page 69

Phrasal verb list *p.117*

7

What are our most important years?

1 Listening

A ▶7.1 In pairs, look at the photos and answer the lesson title. Then listen to the start of an interview. Did you agree with Dr. Castro?

childhood

adolescence

your 20s

your 30s and beyond

B ▶7.2 Note down two reasons Dr. Castro might give to support her opinion. Listen to check. Were any of your ideas mentioned?

C ▶7.2 Listen again. Check (✔) the statements she agrees with.
1. ☐ Society is more forgiving of mistakes you make in your teens.
2. ☐ Your 20s should be a sort of rehearsal for adult life.
3. ☐ It's harder to reinvent yourself in your 30s and 40s.
4. ☐ These days it's relatively easy to succeed in your 20s.

D ▶7.3 Read *Animal idioms*. Then look at the pictures on the right and guess the missing words. Listen to check.

> **Animal idioms**
>
> There are dozens of common English expressions based on animals:
>
> Who **let the cat out of the bag** (= accidentally revealed a secret) about the surprise party?
>
> I know this is true! I heard it **straight from the horse's mouth** (= from a reliable source).
>
> I was planning to go skydiving, but I **chickened out** (= decided not to do it out of fear) at the last minute.

E Make it personal In groups, discuss 1–3.
1. Look at the lesson title again. Did you change your mind after the interview? Why (not)?
2. Which of the idioms from D do you associate with people your age? Your parents' or children's ages? Why?
3. Choose a statement from C you (dis)agree with. Support your opinion with a story about yourself.

> I agree with number 3. You can't teach an old dog new tricks, as they say!

> I totally disagree. My mom went back to school and started a whole new career.

1 _____ a can of worms (= do something that will lead to problems)

2 take the bull by the _____ (= deal with a difficult situation)

3 You can't teach an old dog new _____ (= It's hard to abandon old habits.)

4 get out of the rat _____ (= abandon a competitive lifestyle)

♪ *And isn't it ironic ... don't you think? It's like rain on your wedding day. It's a free ride when you've already paid*

2 Vocabulary: Milestones

A ▶ 7.4 Using context, complete 1–6 with a form of the expressions in the box. Listen to check. Which expression always has a negative meaning?

> come to terms with   come of age   make it through   the stakes are higher
> get off track   take charge

1 Yes, but I would argue that when we _____ (= reach adulthood), we make the decisions that have the greatest impact on our future.
2 Because that's when our lives either take off or _____ (= start to go in the wrong direction).
3 But when you're in your 20s, _____ (= there's more at risk).
4 I _____ (= survived) my 20s, and even the rough times, but I wish I'd been more focused.
5 We need to _____ (= accept) the fact that most of the choices we make in our 20s have life-long consequences.
6 So it's really in your 20s that you need to _____ (= assume control) and determine your destiny.

B In pairs, choose a situation for sentences 1–4. Then role-play a short conversation.
1 "It started well, but it *got off track* halfway through. I nearly fell asleep towards the end."
2 "It's been a year, but I still haven't *come to terms with* the idea that she's left me."
3 "I don't know how I *made it through* the first week. But then I got used to it."
4 "I think he really needs to *take charge* of the situation and try to fix it."

> So, how was the lecture? Did I miss anything important?

> Well, it started well, but it got off track halfway through. I nearly ...

C Complete 1–6 with the expressions in A. Which opinion(s) do you agree with?

WHAT'S THE RIGHT AGE TO GET MARRIED?

→ Not until you're in your 30s. If things don't work out, ¹_____, especially if there are children involved.

→ When a relationship ²_____, couples need to stick together so they can ³_____ the bad times, and that takes a lot of maturity. So I'd say wait until you're in your mid-20s at least.

→ There's no such thing as "the right age." Once you've ⁴_____ and feel you're mature enough to ⁵_____ of your own life without depending on other people, I'd say go for it!

→ I got divorced last year, and I'm still ⁶_____ being on my own again. So, right now, I'm the last person you should ask!

> We met, fell madly in love, got engaged, had a lovely wedding and honeymoon. Then things turned sour, we grew bitter, separated, and divorced. It was quite a busy weekend!

D **Make it personal** In groups, decide on the best ages for these activities. Use expressions from A.

get your child a cell phone   let your child start dating   start learning a foreign language
travel on your own for the first time   have a baby   become a boss   start your own business

> You should be at least 40 before you start your own business.

> Yes, the stakes are much higher when the company is yours!

Common mistakes

(who are)
People ~~at / in / of~~ my age aren't mature enough to have a baby!

are
Couples who ~~have~~ the same age get along best.

7.2 Would you like to live to be 100?

3 Language in use

A ▶7.5 Listen to a sociology professor discuss changing attitudes toward older people. In pairs, answer 1–2.

1. How does he define "ageism"?
2. Is he optimistic or pessimistic about the future?

B ▶7.5 Listen again without looking at the statements below. Then check (✔) the ones you remember Dr. Suárez making to support his prediction of a changing workplace.

1. ☐ By 2050, most of you will have been working for several decades, and you will have developed many valuable skills by that time. You won't be ready to stop.
2. ☐ Nevertheless, some of you will have decided you'd like to spend more time with family.
3. ☐ Many more people will have discovered they can reinvent themselves. The majority of the population will have accepted 60 is the new 40.
4. ☐ The proportion of older workers will have changed because the number of new workers will have slowed considerably.
5. ☐ Society will have been gradually accepting this demographic change, and older workers won't have been fired prematurely.
6. ☐ Older workers also won't have developed the physical limitations they have today.

C In pairs, which statements from B do you agree with? Why (not)? Can you add one more of your own?

> I agree with number 6. Look how far medicine has advanced in the last 50 years.

> Yes, but isn't that wishful thinking? There are limits to how much the aging process can be delayed.

D **Make it personal** What age-related behaviors might be more / less common by 2050?

1. Look at the photos. Do any of today's age-related behaviors surprise you? Make notes.

2. Read *Clarifying opinions*. Then in groups, share your reactions to the photos. Be sure to clarify any ideas your classmates don't seem to understand.

Clarifying opinions

You may use expressions such as *What I mean(t) is that ...*, *What I was trying to say is that ...*, and *Let me put it another way* to clarify opinions you realize were too broad or weren't clear:

Sexism will have disappeared. [very broad]

What I mean is that people will have more open attitudes. [more specific]

> I think many older women will be dating younger men. For one thing, sexism will have disappeared.

> You've got to be kidding! But I do think people won't be aging as quickly, and of course, women will still live longer on average.

> Well, what I mean is that people will have more open attitudes and abandon the old stereotype that the man must be older.

♪ Wherever you go, whatever you do, I will be right here waiting for you

7.2

4 Grammar: Future perfect and future perfect continuous

A Read the grammar box and check (✔) the correct rules (1–3).

Future perfect and future perfect continuous: active and passive

We			**worked**	since our twenties.
			been working	for 50 years by the time we retire.
I	will	have	**seen**	many social changes by then.
People	won't			
These changes			**been accepted**	by the vast majority of people.
Older people			**been forced**	out of the workplace prematurely.

1 The future perfect and continuous ☐ **sometimes** ☐ **never** have the same meaning.
2 When a future event will have ended by the time referred to, use the ☐ **future perfect** ☐ **future perfect continuous**.
3 In passive sentences, use ☐ **either form** ☐ **only the future perfect**.

» **Grammar expansion p.150**

B Underline examples of the future perfect and future perfect continuous in **3B**. Next to each one, write rule numbers 1, 2, or 3.

Common mistake
Even when I'm 90, I won't have ~~been forgetting~~ *forgotten* my English.

C Circle the correct options (1–7). In which two are both choices correct? Which do you agree with?

→ By 2050, every two out of nine people ¹[**will have reached** / **will have been reaching**] the age of 60, and life expectancy ²[**will have exceeded** / **will have been exceeding**] 76 years.
→ The majority of people ³[**will have lived** / **will have been living**] in urban areas for some time.
→ While we ⁴[**won't have stopped** / **won't have been stopping**] aging, health care ⁵[**will have been improving** / **will have been improved**] significantly by then and will be linked to happiness.
→ And, of course, by then, we ⁶[**will have been using** / **will have used**] technology for over 50 years, and our proficiency ⁷[**will have become** / **will have been becoming**] impressive.

5 Pronunciation: Reduction of future forms in informal speech

A ▶ **7.6 and 7.7** Read and listen to the rules. Then listen to and repeat 1–3.

In rapid, informal speech, future perfect forms are often reduced:
will have been = *will /ə/ been*   won't have been = *won't /ə/ been*
In more formal speech, and when a vowel follows, say *will've* and *won('t)'ve*:
will have exceeded = *will /əv/ exceeded*   won't have exceeded = *won't /əv/ exceeded*

1 I will have been working for 50 years and won't have been bored at all.
2 We will have been exposed to many new things.
3 Employers won't have expected people to retire early.

B **Make it personal** The sentences in **4C** are all positive changes. What negative changes can you imagine might take place in the same areas? Use reduced future forms where possible.

life expectancy   cities   health care   social problems   technology

> I predict our online security will have been compromised.

> Yes, the government will have been accessing our personal data for some time.

75

7.3 Do babies ever surprise you?

6 Reading

A Read the first two paragraphs and cover the rest. In pairs, guess the things babies might be capable of.

Five Things You Didn't Know Babies Could Do

Himanshu Sharma

There's simply no better way to put it: babies are essentially vegetables. Sure, they're cute and everything, but at the end of the day, ¹we all know that they're primitive organisms who are yet to develop the basic functions to qualify as cognitive human beings. As the babies grow, they will slowly develop various functions necessary to survive in the world.

But as research is gradually finding out, ²babies are capable of much more than we usually give them credit for.

5 Distinguishing faces, even of other species

If you've ever spent time with a baby, you'll know that they're not so great at recognizing people by their faces. They don't seem to behave in a particularly different way when they see someone they have met earlier, unless it's their mother or someone they spend a lot of time with. The ability to tell faces apart from each other is something they acquire much later in their lives. ³Or that's what the babies would rather have you believe, anyway.

Babies are actually pretty good at identifying faces, even when it comes to creatures of different species. In an experiment conducted by researchers at the University of Sheffield and University of London, six-month-old babies were found to be as good as adults at recognizing human faces that they had seen earlier. But, shockingly, they were actually better at recognizing monkey faces than the adults. How many of us can tell monkeys apart by their faces? We bet it's not a lot. Yet, apparently, six-month-old babies can do just that. We lose the ability to recognize the faces of different species and races as we grow older, because an adult's facial recognition is based more on familiarity than absolute facial indicators, but babies still carry this vestigial ability up to a certain age.

4 Judging character

⁴The ability to judge how likely someone is to help you comes built in as an evolutionary trait. It's a social skill that's essential to operating in a society as well as to survival. This was especially true during the hunter-gatherer times, when knowing if someone was likely to kill you and steal your belongings was pretty helpful. It's a crucial ability, and—surprisingly enough—one that comes with the package at birth instead of being developed over years of social communication, as we're generally inclined to assume.

Researchers set up an experiment and made some babies watch a puppet show. One puppet was shown to be climbing a mountain, while the second and third puppet would either help the climber up or throw him back down, respectively. When the babies were offered the last two puppets, 14 out of 16 10-month-olds and all 12 six-month-olds preferred the helper over the hinderer. While researchers still don't know whether it's an informed decision, ⁵drooling infants seemingly staring blankly at things sure register far more information than we knew.

3 Learning language in the womb

Learning a whole new language is a process that takes a long time to perfect, especially when it comes to conversing in a social environment. The verbal cues, gestures, subtle winks, and other aspects of communicating take years to master. While it is something that we get better at as we grow older, this development starts much earlier than you'd think: before you're even born.

Babies apparently learn their native language from their mothers in the womb and can identify their mother tongue when they're barely hours old. Researchers recorded the vowel sounds in the native tongues of some 30-hour-old babies and studied their reactions to see if they recognized the sounds. The researchers plugged a pacifier into a computer and made the babies suck on it. Sucking for a shorter period of time meant that the sound was familiar, and vice versa. As it turned out, the babies appeared to recognize the sounds played in their mother tongue, indicating that we're born with at least a rudimentary sense of what our native language sounds like.

♪ I hear babies crying. I watch them grow. They'll learn much more than I'll ever know. And I think to myself, What a wonderful world

7.3

2 Understanding social interactions

In our daily lives, we often need to know the context of a social interaction to respond accordingly. The mind can collate data on what's going on around you and suggest the best course of action based on that information. Of course, babies can't do that, but they do know the basics of social communication.

Researchers studied babies between 24 and 120 hours of age. They employed a technique known as near-infrared spectroscopy to monitor the part of the brain responsible for social interactions. What they found was that this section of the brain lit up in response to a real social interaction—facial expressions, social gestures, and so on—but did not respond to, say, an arm manipulating a random object. ⁶This suggests that babies are wired to recognize social clues from birth.

There had been similar studies on older babies before, but this was the first time social interactions were studied in babies as young as 24 hours. Interestingly, the older babies were better at successfully differentiating the various types of communication, suggesting that this ability rapidly develops in the early stages of life.

1 Fairness

Our sense of fairness is something that probably helps us save a ton of money by not getting ripped off all the time. It's no surprise that we have it; it's an evolved mechanism that lets us function in a social environment. But what is a surprise is how early we develop this crucial ability. According to science, babies as young as 15 months are able to distinguish a fair deal from an unfair one.

Babies were made to sit on their parents' laps and look at a video of someone distributing food to two people. This was done twice. The first time, the food was distributed equally. The second time, one recipient got more food than the other. The babies were more surprised and hence stared longer at the unfair transaction compared to when the food was divided equally. ⁷Even if a baby's basic sense of fairness isn't much use for either the baby or anyone else, it's surprising that this ability starts developing way before it's actually needed in life.

B ▶ 7.8 Read and listen to the article. In pairs, recall explanation for each skill babies have. Were you surprised?

> It seems logical babies would be better at recognizing faces.

C Re-read and, in pairs, explain the author's opinions in the numbered sentences 1–7. Replace the blue highlighted expressions with a similar meaning.

> In sentence 1, he's saying that everyone thinks babies still haven't developed cognitive functions.

D 🌐 **Make it personal** Search on "Things babies can do." What other surprising things did you discover?

> Did you know babies can yell at birth, but not cry? Tears can't be formed until they're about three weeks old.

7 Vocabulary: Adjective-noun collocations in writing and speech

A Read *Finding common adjective-noun collocations*. Find the underlined collocations with *social* in context. Which are you familiar with?

> **Finding common adjective-noun collocations**
>
> News sources often use adjective-noun collocations that are common in conversation. For example:
>
> It's a *social skill* that's essential.

B Make it personal Have you ever felt you weren't treated appropriately for your age? Look at the highlighted adjective-noun collocations in the article. Then use them and the collocations from A to share stories in groups.

> My parents didn't even have a rudimentary sense of how teenagers think. For example, when it came to social interactions, they didn't seem to remember peer pressure.

77

7.4 Do you seem younger or older than you are?

8 Language in use

A ▶ 7.9 Listen to the start of a community lecture. Complete the notes.

- Nature vs. nurture: the influence of ¹_____ vs. ²_____.
- Stage theorists vs. others: development is ³_____ vs. it's affected by ⁴_____.

B ▶ 7.10 Read the quotes from the street interviews. Then listen to the rest of the lecture. Match the people in the order you hear them (1–6) to their photos.

WHAT IS "AGE-APPROPRIATE" BEHAVIOR?

A ☐☐ It's my grandmother who walks two miles a day. And she's pushing 90!

B ☐☐ It's my younger brother who's more mature. He's wise beyond his years.

C ☐☐ We're not the ones who will reform society. We seem to have run out of ideas and just conform to expectations.

D ☐☐ Act my age? No way! It's a crazy situation I find myself in now. I'm the one who puts food on the table.

E 1 ☐ My teacher is in her early 70s, and she's really young at heart. It's my classmates who seem old-fashioned.

F ☐☐ It's not old people who are boring. They have so much insight and first-hand experience. It's us!

C ▶ 7.10 Listen again. Match opinions a–d to the six people in B. Did anyone surprise you?

a Nature is more important than nurture.
b Nurture is more important than nature.
c Stage theory is usually accurate.
d People simply don't fit into neat stages.

D In pairs, explain the meaning of the highlighted expressions in context.

> I think to be pushing 90 means "she's almost 90." If you think about the meaning of *push*, it makes sense!

E Make it personal What are your views on human development?

1 In groups, choose opinions from B. Note down examples from your life or the lives of others.
2 Share a story about yourself or someone you know to illustrate your views. Use expressions from A.

> I'd say life stages are unpredictable, and I have first-hand experience, too! People my age might be in college, but I dropped out to become a singer.

> What convinced you to do it?

♪ If you ever get close to a human, And human behavior. Be ready, be ready to get confused

7.4

9 Grammar: Cleft sentences

A Read the grammar box. Write S (subject) or O (object) next to each sentence. What clue gave you the answer? Then find five cleft sentences in 8B. Write S or O next to each.

Cleft sentences: subject and object focus

It's	older people	who / that	have a perspective on life. [1]
	your attitude	that	has to change. [2]
	not how long you live		always determines your savings. [3]
	saving now		will pay off later. [4]
	an unusual phase of life	(that)	we find ourselves in. [5]
	a tough situation		we have to face. [6]
	a way of dealing with the future		he's looking for. [7]

A cleft sentence can focus on a subject or object:
Subject: *Your attitude* has to change. → It's your attitude that has to change.
Object: We have to face *a tough situation*. → It's a tough situation (that) we have to face.

» Grammar expansion p.150

B Rewrite the underlined parts of Leo's responses (1–6) as cleft sentences.

Does anything tend to bother you, Leo?

Yes, when I see people not acting their age, it really bothers me. ¹I'm not bothered by their behavior, as such. But ²my expectations aren't being met. For example, if I see an 80-year-old on a skateboard, ³the complete surprise leaves me speechless. I guess you could say, ⁴I just haven't expected a sight [like that]. As for what bothers me, ⁵I think I feel envy. If I can't skateboard now, how will I skateboard at 80? ⁶My own fears are getting in the way of positive thoughts!

1 It's not their behavior, as such, that bothers me.

C Read *Alternatives to cleft sentences*. Find two alternatives in 8B.

Alternatives to cleft sentences

Cleft sentences with pronouns may sound unnatural and, at times, even ungrammatical when the pronoun is a subject. Instead, use *the one(s)*:

~~It's not him~~ who wants to change jobs. → He's not the one who wants to change jobs.

D Change the underlined responses (1–4) using alternatives to cleft sentences.

A: Why did you borrow money from your parents?
B: ¹I didn't borrow money.
A: What do you mean?
B: ²They borrowed $200 from me. They're really not acting their age!
A: What's it got to do with age? And besides, aren't they out of work?
B: ³I need the money. I want to buy a car.
A: ⁴Maybe you're not acting your age. You're only 17!

E **Make it personal** In pairs, discuss 1–3. Use cleft sentences (and alternatives) where possible.

1 Do you agree with the opinions in 8C?
2 Do you know any adults who don't act their age?
3 Do you think parents are at fault when children don't act their age?

> Are parents at fault when children don't act their age?

> Yes, because it's their parents that don't set expectations.

7.5 What would your ideal job be?

10 Listening

A ▶ 7.11 Listen to Mia talking to her friend Jack about having a younger boss. Complete the missing words (1–5) in Bill's suggestions.

1. Maybe it's time for some new _____.
2. It's your age you have to take out of the _____.
3. Just relax, be yourself, but still show _____.
4. He also might appreciate your _____ information with him.
5. You're the one who has the most to _____ if you help him solve his problems.

B In pairs, what do these expressions from A mean?

1. "take [something] out of the _____"
2. "[you] have the most to _____"

C ▶ 7.12 Listen to the next part of the conversation. Complete the chart.

	Mia	Her boss, Tim
Character traits	1	4
Qualifications	2	5
Experience	3	6

▶ 7.13 Listen to Mia and her boss. Check (✔) 1, 2, or 3. Do you think Jack's advice made a difference?

Tim becomes interested in what Mia is saying because …

1. ☐ she asks his advice.   2. ☐ she presents a solution.   3. ☐ both 1 and 2.

11 Keep talking

A In pairs, brainstorm jobs you feel you're ideally suited for, but where you might be seen as too young (or old).

1. Plan two reasons for each category: character traits, qualifications, and experience.
2. Counter the argument about your age with reasons from 1.

B ▶ 7.14 **How to say it** Complete the chart. Listen to check.

Formal requests	
What they said	What they meant
1 I hope I'm not _____ .	You might be busy.
2 I had an idea for the report I wanted to _____ by you.	I want to know what you think.
3 _____ it be OK if I went ahead?	Can I go ahead?
4 I wonder if I could _____ work at home tomorrow.	I'd like to work at home tomorrow.
5 Would you be so _____ as to close the door?	Please close the door.

C Imagine you got the job in A. Role-play a conversation with your boss and ask to work on an important project. Use *How to say it* expressions.

> May I come in for a minute? I hope I'm not …

> Yes, by all means.

> I had an idea I wanted to … by you. I wonder if I could … work on the … project? You know I'm very … so I thought I'd be perfect for it.

♪ Workin' 9 to 5. What a way to make a livin'. Barely gettin' by. It's all takin' and no givin'

7.5

12 Writing: A job-application letter

A Read the letter. Then identify …
1 five positive character traits the writer mentions.
2 two qualifications for the job.
3 one example of her past experience.
4 three specific responsibilities she's had.

General Director, Meliá Hotels
April 12, 2017

Dear Sir or Madam:

1 ¹_____ your online ad of March 31, where you posted an opening for an entry-level receptionist in your hotel chain. ²_____ the position, and am attaching my résumé.

2 Having graduated from Anhembi Morumbi University in São Paulo with a BA in Hotel Management, I am eager to put my skills to use. ³_____ my résumé, I speak four languages fluently: English (my native language), Portuguese, Spanish, and German. Therefore, I believe my profile ⁴_____ in one of the São Paulo branches of the Meliá Hotels group. However, I'm open to opportunities in Rio de Janeiro, as well.

3 Working in your prestigious hotel chain would be rewarding work for me. I have excellent communication skills and am attentive to detail. In addition, I enjoy interacting with customers and serving their needs. In several summer jobs where I've worked as an assistant in reception, I have been praised as dynamic and pro-active. My past responsibilities have included problem-solving room assignments, checking in customers, and answering routine questions. ⁵_____, I have learned to interact with a wide variety of people from many backgrounds and nationalities. Helping customers has strengthened my desire to have a future career in hotel management.

4 While I am aware this would be my first full-time hotel assignment, I consider myself a quick learner. My academic background has familiarized me with many aspects of the hotel industry. On-the-job experience would allow me to translate the theoretical to the practical.

5 ⁶_____. Thank you very much in advance.

Sincerely,
Linda Baker

Common mistake

Working there would be a ~~rewarding~~ work for me. *(rewarding)*

B Read *Formulaic expressions (2)*. Then complete 1–6 in the letter with the expressions given.

Formulaic expressions (2)

Formulaic expressions like these are commonly used in job-application letters.
I believe I am highly suited to (this sort of assignment).
As you will see on (p.2) / in (the attached sample) …
In this capacity, (I answered phones).
I am writing in response to (your job opening).
I hope you will give my (résumé) careful consideration.
(I) would be a perfect fit for (this job).

C Read *Write it right!* In paragraphs 3 and 4, underline two more examples of sentences beginning with noun phrases and one of a sentence beginning with an *-ing* form.

Write it right!

Job-application letters are fairly short and often include sentences beginning with …
1 noun phrases as subjects:
My past responsibilities have included problem-solving …
2 *-ing* forms used as nouns, as opposed to sentences beginning with *it*, which take longer to get to the point:
Working in your prestigious hotel would be rewarding work for me.

D Change 1–4 into sentences beginning with an *-ing* form. What kind of job might each person be applying for?
1 It would be fulfilling to use my writing skills.
2 It was responding to emergencies that taught me to make rapid decisions.
3 It was studying linguistics that helped me develop an interest in computing language.
4 It would be the dream of a lifetime to work at such a world-famous hospital.

E **Your turn!** Choose a job you brainstormed in **11A** and write a job-application letter in about 280 words.

Before
List the character traits, qualifications, and experience that make you an excellent candidate.

While
Write four to five paragraphs, following the model in **A**. Use formulaic expressions and begin sentences with noun phrases (including *-ing* forms).

After
Post your letter online and read your classmates' work. Whose letter is most convincing?

8
What makes a restaurant special?

1 Listening

A ▶8.1 Listen to the start of a lecture on business practices. Which picture (1–2) does the speaker imply the dinner will be like?

B ▶8.2 In pairs, guess what happened next. Listen to check. Then answer 1–3.
1 Who came to the dinner?
2 What were they given at the end?
3 What was the true reason for the dinner?

C ▶8.2 Listen again. What do 1–4 mean in context? Choose a or b.
1 bland   a ☐ smooth, not irritating   b ☐ tasteless
2 shrug off   a ☐ not care   b ☐ brush off, remove
3 baffled   a ☐ puzzled   b ☐ frustrated
4 oblivious to   a ☐ unaffected by   b ☐ unaware of

D ▶8.3 Listen to the last part. Why didn't the companies sue the site? Check (✔) the correct answer.
1 ☐ They probably wouldn't succeed.
2 ☐ It probably wasn't in their interest.
3 ☐ both 1 and 2

E Make it personal Does advertising work? In groups, discuss 1–3.
1 How effective do you think campaigns like the one described in **A** really are?

> Very effective! These days any video offering the unexpected goes viral almost immediately.

2 Which quotes (a–f) do you like most / least? Why? Take a class vote.

> a "The only people who care about advertising are the people who work in advertising." (George Parker)
>
> b "Don't find customers for your product. Find products for your customers." (Seth Godin)
>
> c "Advertisers constantly invent cures to which there is no disease." (Author unknown)
>
> d "Ads sell a great deal more than products. They sell values, images, and concepts of success and worth." (Brené Brown)
>
> e "Advertising teaches people not to trust their judgment. Advertising teaches people to be stupid." (Carl Sagan)
>
> f "Let's gear our advertising to sell our goods, but let's recognize also that advertising has a broad social responsibility." (Leo Burnett)

3 Guess why the quotes were all written by men. Similar opinions?

♪ No one learned from your mistakes. We let our profits go to waste. All that's left in any case, Is advertising space

8.1

2 Vocabulary: Expressions with *take* for discussing events

A ▶ 8.4 Listen to excerpts 1–6. When you hear the "beep", say one of the expressions below. Use the correct form of *take*. Continue listening to check.

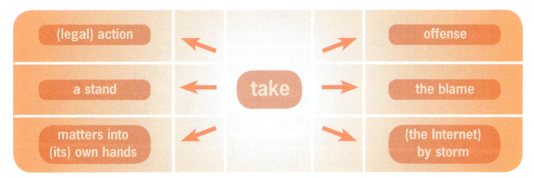

B 🛜 In groups, use your instincts to guess the correct preposition (1–4). Search on the expression to check. Then change the sentences so they're true for you.
1 I wish more people would take a stand [**about** / **against**] GM foods.
2 In my country, it's easy to take legal action [**over** / **against**] cyber stalkers.
3 I take offense [**at** / **with**] jokes aimed at minority groups.
4 I sometimes get into trouble at work because I take the blame [**for** / **of**] my colleagues' mistakes.

C ▶ 8.5 Listen to two friends, Gary and Ruth, talking about a nightmare purchase. Take notes on 1–5. Then answer using expressions from **A**.
1 How popular does Ruth think a campaign like that would be in the U.S.?
2 How did Gary react when Ruth mentioned the old washing machine?
3 Whose fault was the wrong delivery?
4 How apologetic was the manager?
5 What does Gary say he might do in the end?

D Make it personal Talk about bad service!
1 ▶ 8.6 **How to say it** Complete the chart. Listen to check.

Describing negative experiences	
What they said	What they meant
1 On _____ of that, (it took them three days to get back to me).	To make a bad situation worse or more painful ...
2 To make _____ worse, (she said it was the delivery company's fault).	
3 As if that were not _____, (they charged my credit card again).	
4 To _____ insult to injury, (they didn't even apologize).	

2 What was the worst experience you've ever had at a restaurant? Think through a–b and make notes.
  a the most relevant details (What / Where / When / Who / Why / How long)
  b the outcome and what you learned from the experience
3 In groups, share your stories. Use *How to say it* expressions and ones with *take*. Who had the worst experience?

Common mistakes
The food was ~~tasteful~~ / tasteless. *(tasty)*
The decoration was ~~tasty~~ / tasteless. *(tasteful)*

> I once had to wait an hour before my order was taken, so I took matters into my own hands.

> What did you do? Grab food from the kitchen?

> I stood up and yelled "Fire." So to add insult to injury, they accused me of creating a disturbance!

8.2 Are you a demanding customer?

3 Language in use

A Read the cartoon. Do you agree? What advice would you give the waitress?

B ▶8.7 Listen to Raúl and his private English tutor, Julia. Check (✔) the problems with his text.
- ☐ There are a few grammar mistakes.
- ☐ It's too wordy.
- ☐ It's too formal.
- ☐ The vocabulary is too simple.

C ▶8.8 Listen to the next part of their conversation. Underline the sentences in sections 1–4 of Raúl's draft handout that Julia suggests changing. Which reason in B does she give?

> **Guidelines for dealing with complaints – draft**
> Once you realize that a customer is dissatisfied, try to imagine yourself in his or her position, even if you're not to blame. Then follow these four easy guidelines:
> 1. It is critically important that your customers communicate how they feel. They need time and space to express their dissatisfaction. Then, apologize – even if you feel their criticism is unfair.
> 2. Listen actively. It is essential that you not draw any conclusions until you know all the facts. Then repeat your customer's concerns to make sure you have correctly identified the key issues.
> 3. If you can respond to the issue at hand immediately, do it. It is crucial that problems be resolved quickly.
> 4. A customer may insist that he or she speak to the manager. If that happens, try to find someone in a position of authority to support you.

D ▶8.8 Try to remember Julia's suggested changes. Cross out the words and write the new ones in Raúl's handout. Then listen again to check. Did you get them all?

E Make it personal In pairs, discuss 1–3. Similar opinions?
1. Which of Raúl's guidelines in C should companies follow more often? Would you add any others?
2. Should businesses refund or exchange damaged products with "no questions asked"?
3. Do you notice the writing style of letters businesses send? How informal should it be?

> I'd add that a salesperson shouldn't answer the phone when the customer is talking!

♪ Oh cherie amour, pretty little one that I adore. You're the only girl my heart beats for. How I wish that you were mine

8.2

4 Grammar: The subjunctive

A Read the grammar box and check (✔) the correct rules (a–c). Then, without looking back at 3B, rephrase the underlined parts of 1–4 using the subjunctive. Use the word in parentheses.

The subjunctive: verbs and expressions with *it's*

I wish		the shirt were	on sale.
I demanded		he give	me a refund.
I insist	(that)	the manager see	me right now.
I suggest		we look into	this matter.
It was important		you not be	rude.
It's essential		she research	her purchase.

a After *wish*, the subjunctive form for *he* and *she* is ☐ **was** ☐ **were**.
b After other verbs, and expressions with *it's*, the subjunctive is the ☐ **base** ☐ **past tense** form.
c When the first verb is in the past, the subjunctive form ☐ **changes** ☐ **doesn't change**.

» Grammar expansion p.152

1 <u>It's important for your customers to say</u> how they feel. (important)
2 <u>Don't jump to any conclusions</u> until you know all the facts. (essential)
3 <u>Problems must be resolved</u> quickly. (crucial)
4 A customer <u>may want to speak</u> to the manager. (insist)

B Read *Using the subjunctive*. Then complete 1–6 below. Imagine a context for each.

Using the subjunctive

The subjunctive is relatively uncommon in English, and is used in formal speech and writing. In conversation, other structures are frequently used:
It's important **for you not to be** rude. / **Please don't be** rude.
They suggested **speaking** to you. / They **said to speak** to you.

Plain English: All it's cracked up to be?

Writers often recommend a communication style that's short, clear, and to the point. But are we going too far in that direction? In this course, you'll learn how to make your language more emphatic – useful skills for writing and formal speeches.

Instead of:
1 Do your best to meet the deadline.
2 Don't be late.
3 He should seek help immediately.
4 I'm sorry Dad isn't here to witness this day.
5 All the requirements must be met.
6 She said the contract had to be revised.

It might be better to say:
It's important ... the deadline.
It's essential ... late.
I suggest ... help immediately.
I wish ... here to witness this day.
It's crucial ...
She demanded ...

I think in number 6, some lawyers might be talking about a client.

Common mistake
(that) he take
She suggested ~~him to take~~ legal action.

C Make it personal Be convincing!
1 Choose at least one sentence from the right column of B, decide a context, and plan a short speech. Note down at most five key points.
2 In groups, deliver your speeches. Whose points were clearest? Who sounded the most formal?

Thank you very much for joining me here today. As I think most of you know, I'm the new school director. I'd like to begin by ...

85

8.3 What are the worst aspects of air travel?

5 Reading

A Read the title. Does Barbara Apple Sullivan expect to be treated well? What clue is there? Read the first four paragraphs to check.

B 🌐 In pairs, guess why Barbara had a "reinvigorated customer experience." Then read the rest to check. Make certain you understand the highlighted words, and search online for images, if necessary.

> I think she might have been given a free flight ...

The True Story Of Amazing Customer Service From – Gasp! – An Airline

1 When Barbara Apple Sullivan acci**den**tally dropped her passport in a Charles de Gaulle airport mailbox just before boarding a flight, she was certain she'd be stuck for days. But thanks to a Delta employee, she made it on board and had her future travel plans transformed forever.

2 **"Keep Climbing."**

That is the slogan for Delta Airlines' latest advertising campaign, which highlights its promise for a "rein**vig**orated customer experience." So often I have seen this television commercial and others like it, paying little attention to the message and the value propo**si**tion. My only takeaway was reas**sur**ance that the planes were pointed upward and not downward.

3 In such a s**at**urated industry, it is difficult for any airline to differ**en**tiate the customer experience. The planes themselves are virtually identical. The food, if it exists, is universally awful. Airport security is conducted by an **en**tity over which the airlines have virtually no control. And virtually everyone who flies has a personal horror story. Is it really possible to redefine the customer experience?

4 It was my personal experience with a single employee that emblazoned Delta's value proposition in my mind forever. Their promise came to life in a real, tangible way. More than any advertising, more than an im**pact**ful website, more than those tasty biscotti cookies served on the plane, this really was a reinvigorated customer experience.

5 Allow me to set the scene. To my horror, I inad**ver**tently dropped my passport in a mailbox at Charles de Gaulle airport last Sunday morning (it was bundled with all my VAT refund envelopes). The instant the mail left my hand and dropped to the bottom of the mailbox, I realized my error. Two airport employees told me it was impossible to open the mailbox on a Sunday since postal workers, who do not work on Sundays, have sole authority to open the box. I was told I must wait until Monday, go to the U.S. Embassy in Paris, and request an emergency passport before I would be able to fly. In despe**ra**tion, I approached the Delta ticket counter and told them I had a BIG problem.

One gentleman behind the counter, Mr. Karim Sayoud, took my problem as though it were his own. He calmed me in my increasing panic, explained what he could do and immediately called the U.S. Homeland Security Customs and Border Control repre**sen**tative station at the airport.

Mr. James Wilkinson from U.S. Homeland Security came to in**ter**rogate me. All I had was my passport number. I had nothing else. No copy of my passport, no social security card, and the address on my driver's license did not match my passport. After providing enough correct answers to convince him that I was in fact who I said I was, he agreed to let me travel, subject to the French authorities that re**tain** final approval.

Karim Sayoud left his position at the Delta ticket counter, es**cort**ed me to Delta check-in, and he convinced his colleagues to accept my baggage (without the certainty that I would be on the flight) and issue a boarding pass. He then escorted me through French passport control and security, encouraging the authorities to let me through, and ul**ti**mately to the Delta gate agents. It was there that I was finally able to breathe a sigh of re**lief**.

Sayoud didn't stop there. After I was successfully on the flight, <u>he took it upon himself</u> to make certain that my passport was re**trieved** from the mailbox the following day and returned to me in New York. He actually taped a handwritten note on the mailbox so the postal worker would see it and return the passport to Delta once it was retrieved. He phoned and emailed me multiple times each day updating me on the s**ta**tus. Lo and behold, my passport arrived at my address by FedEx – a true customer-service miracle made entirely possible by one de**di**cated employee.

—Barbara Apple Sullivan, is CEO and a managing partner of Sullivan, a multidisciplinary brand-engagement firm based in New York City. Follow them on Twitter at @sullivannyc

♪ You've got a friend in me. When the road looks rough ahead, And you're miles and miles, From your nice warm bed

8.3

C ▶ 8.9 Listen to and re-read the article. T (true) or F (false)? Correct the false statements.
1 Barbara accidentally dropped her passport in a mailbox when she was mailing letters.
2 Airport employees in Paris are allowed to open mailboxes if they have the keys.
3 Karim Sayoud first tried to reassure Barbara and then had a security and border-control representative interview her.
4 Whether Barbara was allowed to fly was ultimately up to U.S. Homeland Security.
5 Karim Sayoud took multiple steps to make sure Barbara got her passport back.

D Make it personal In pairs, how unusual do you think Barbara's story is? If you'd had the same experience at an airport, train, or bus station, would you have gotten the same level of help? Why (not)?

> If this had happened to me, it wouldn't have occurred to me to ask Delta for help.

6 Vocabulary: Expressions of help

A Read *Describing helpful behaviour*. Then cover the chart and use the cues 1–6 to retell Karim's story.

Describing helpful behaviour

Common expressions of help, like the one underlined in the text, often have similar meanings.

Karim Sayoud	took it upon himself went to great lengths went out of his way went the extra mile moved mountains	to make	sure Barbara got her passport.
	took it from there	and made	
	saw to it that	she was fully satisfied.	

1 When Karim learned about the problem, he [take / upon / himself] to …
2 He then [go / extra / mile], left the counter, and …
3 He [move / mountains] to make sure the authorities …
4 On Monday, he [take / from / there] and saw to it that Barbara's passport …
5 He [go / out / way] and even … for a postal worker.
6 He then [go / great / lengths] to keep Barbara updated and …

B Make it personal Share stories about Good Samaritans.
1 The unlucky people in the pictures were all helped by thoughtful people. In pairs, share what you think happened, using expressions from A.

a

b

c

2 Has a stranger ever gone out of his / her way for you? Or vice versa? In groups, share your stories. Whose is the most remarkable?

> A guy I'd never met before really went to great lengths for me once and …

87

8.4 Have you ever borrowed money?

7 Language in use

A ▶8.10 Listen to two friends, Alba and Paul, discussing bureaucracy. In pairs, answer 1–2.

1. What was the problem?
2. Guess what Alba decided to do.

B ▶8.11 Listen to the complete conversation. Match the comments with the topics (a–f). There's one extra.

1. As much as you might try to plan your life, there are always unpleasant surprises.
2. However generous he may have been, for us it was a nightmare.
3. Whatever compromises you feel are reasonable, none will be convincing.
4. For all the good arguments you come up with, they just won't budge.
5. As exciting as it sounds, some things just aren't worth it.

a ☐ paying taxes
b ☐ getting an inheritance
c ☐ having a lot of money
d ☐ Spanish bureaucracy
e ☐ government bureaucrats
f ☐ Alba's uncle's restaurant

8 Vocabulary: Words for discussing money

A Read *Money terms*. Then complete 1–6 below with a form of the words in the box.

> **Money terms**
>
> Terms involving money can vary quite a bit across languages. For example, the Spanish verb *cobrar* can mean "to charge (an amount)," "to get paid (a salary)," "to cash (a check)," or "to collect (a debt)." In English, these are all separate verbs. Always learn money terms in context. A noun and a verb may be identical or have different forms.
>
> "I'm afraid they're going to *tax* (v.) me a lot this year." "The *tax* (n.) is very high, too."
> Tom might *inherit* (v.) a lot of money. He's going to have a big *inheritance* (n.)

| borrow   charge (n. / v.)   inherit   loan (n. / v.)   profit (n. / v.)   tax (n. / v.) |

1. *Stand by Us* Electronics has terrible customer service, but they sure make a nice _____ .
2. If I _____ a lot of money, I'd quit my job the next day.
3. Never go to that store on Fourth Street. They _____ me double for a purchase last week. I think they did it on purpose.
4. Ever since the recession, it's really hard to get a _____ . I don't think I'll be able to buy a house – there's so much red tape!
5. I never let people _____ my computer, even if they beg me to!
6. A great state to shop in is Delaware. There's no state _____ .

B Make it personal In groups, discuss 1–2. Any memorable stories?

1. Have you ever had a very (un)pleasant experience with red tape or bureaucracy? What was the situation?
2. Do you know of anyone whose life changed after inheriting money? Any interesting stories?

> Yes, I had an uncle who became a well-known painter. When he no longer had to work, he started to spend his whole day taking art courses.

> I sure wish I could do that!

88

♪ It's a bittersweet symphony, this life. Try to make ends meet. You're a slave to the money, then you die

8.4

9 Grammar: Adverb clauses to emphasize conditions or contrasts

A Read the grammar box and complete the rules (a–c).

Adverb clauses to emphasize conditions or contrasts		
1 **However** reasonable the price	**may** seem,	the watch still doesn't work.
2 **Whatever** discount you	**might** give me,	it won't be sufficient.
3 **As useful as** the manual	**may** be,	it isn't helping.
4 **(As) much as** you	**try** to please customers,	you're not succeeding.
5 **For all the** help you	**give** me,	I won't shop here again.

a Sentences 1–3 use the modal verbs _____ or _____ to express a condition.
b A condition can also be expressed using the _____ tense.
c Conditions or contrasts with *whatever* are followed by _____, whereas ones with *however* are often followed by _____ or adverbs.

» Grammar expansion p.152

B Write the numbers from the grammar box (1–5) next to the sentences in **7B**. Then rephrase each one so it begins with *No matter* …

No matter how much you might try to plan your life …

Common mistake

~~However the price seems low,~~ *low the price seems*
it's too high!

C Choose the correct answer (1–5) to emphasize a condition or contrast.

¹[**As important as / as much as**] it may be to be polite to customers, sometimes sales people are downright rude. However, anyone who has ever been to Japan knows that employees there have a few things to teach us. ²[**However / Whatever**] annoyed they may feel privately, you would never know it as the customer. ³[**Whatever / For all the**] questions you may have, they will always be answered with a smile. The reason is simple. ⁴[**For all the / As much as**] you may think it is unnatural or even super-human to be so polite, it is actually good for business. How do we know this? By asking customers, of course! ⁵[**However / Whatever**] surveys we've done on customer-service quality, Japan always comes out on top!

D Make it personal Discuss customer service where you live.

1 Check (✔) the customer-service quality for your city for each kind of business. In groups, defend your choice. Use adverb clauses to emphasize conditions or contrasts, where possible.

Customer-service quality	Poor	Average	Good	Excellent
car dealers				
banks				
cell-phone carriers				
clothing stores				
electric companies				

2 Reach a consensus and share it with the class. How many groups agree?

Cell-phone carriers are the worst. Whatever problem you might have, they try to convince you it's your own fault.

Oh, but I've actually had a good experience with [name of company].

8.5 What was the last complaint you made?

10 Listening

A ▶8.12 Listen to the start of Amber's call to a phone company. What's the problem? Guess what she says next.

B ▶8.13 Listen to part two. When you hear "beep," choose Amber's response and write the number. Continue listening to check. There's one extra choice.

a ☐ You mean you save these conversations? I must have made a mistake. But could you please try to accommodate me?
b ☐ Could you please check if there's an earlier opening? It's essential that it be taken care of today.
c ☐ I have an important deadline. I'm not going to be home on May 12.
d ☐ I'd like to wait if at all possible. I'm really quite worried about this.
e ☐ However limited the number may be, it's really important that you find a solution.

C ▶8.14 Guess the polite responses 1–5. Then listen to part three and circle the ones you actually hear. Which words make them rude in this context? Why did the speakers use this tone?

1 Mr. Bell [**says** / **claims**] you recorded me.
2 I need my phone connected [**immediately** / **as soon as possible**].
3 [**I've already provided** / **I believe you have**] this information.
4 [**I'd really appreciate your accommodating** / **I insist that you accommodate**] me.
5 [**Could you possibly speak more softly?** / **I suggest you lower your voice**].

> In the first one, Amber had made a mistake with the date, but she doesn't really believe it. So the word ...

D Make it personal In pairs, discuss 1–2.
1 Who do you sympathize with more, Amber or Ms. McGuire?
2 Were you surprised by the outcome? Why (not)? Would it be different where you live?

> I sympathize with Amber. It's natural to be upset after so many calls!

11 Keep talking

A Choose a type of business where you would like to have a real problem resolved. Note down the details. Be sure to include ...

1 the problem.
2 the steps you've already taken.
3 what exactly you'd like the company to do.
4 what action you'll take if they don't.

store   bank   company   car dealer

B Plan your phone call. Individually, review expressions from 10B and C, and try to imagine the conversation.

C In groups of three, role-play the conversation. Which of you should work for a phone company?
1 **A:** Place the call.
   B: Respond as an employee.
   C: Evaluate whether **A** and **B** are convincing and give suggestions for improvement.
2 Change roles until all the phone calls have been made. Choose one to share with the class.

> [name of business] May I help you?

> Yes, I'm calling concerning a problem I've had with (a purchase) ...

♪ I'm in the phone booth, it's the one across the hall. If you don't answer, I'll just ring it off the wall

12 Writing: A complaint letter

A Read Jacob Banks's complaint letter and match paragraphs 1–5 to their main function.

- [ ] give an opinion on the company's practices
- [ ] introduce the topic and create sympathy
- [ ] document evidence of previous steps
- [ ] make a strong request
- [ ] fully describe a problem

B Match the formal expressions 1–10 in the letter with these more informal ones with a similar meaning.

- [ ] you can help me
- [ ] even though
- [ ] I could easily have given
- [ ] I don't have to do that
- [ ] fix(ed) things (two expressions)
- [ ] If I'm not happy
- [ ] please write back
- [ ] take you to court
- [ ] without success

C Read *Write it right!* Then find two more passive expressions in paragraph 3 that both have the same meaning.

> **Write it right!**
>
> Complaint letters use formal expressions in the passive that mean "I was told," but which avoid mentioning the person who gave the information:
>
> **I was convinced (that)** the problem would be resolved promptly.

D In paragraphs 4 and 5, find …

1. an example of a formal way to express a condition.
2. two examples of the subjunctive.

E **Your turn!** Choose a consumer problem you brainstormed in **11A** and write a formal complaint in about 280 words.

Before
Plan the main function of each paragraph. Note down very specific details on the problem and what steps you've already taken.

While
Write five to six paragraphs to support your complaint, following the model in **A**. Use passive expressions from *Write it right!*, some formal expressions from **B**, and formal structures from **D**.

After
Post your complaint online and read your classmates' work. Whose letter got the most sympathy?

Ms. Eleanor Fernández
Director of Customer Service

Dear Ms. Fernández:

1 I am writing concerning the cancellation of my credit card on September 5, 2016. I have tried repeatedly, but [1]to no avail, to [2]resolve the matter with your staff. I am a college student, and as this is my first and only credit card, I am hopeful [3]you will be able to assist me.

2 On September 1, I attempted to pay my monthly bill of $355.66, but mistakenly authorized a payment of $3355.66. Within a day, my checking account was frozen because of an overdraft, and my credit card was suspended. While my bank immediately [4]rectified the problem, canceling payment and authorizing a new payment in the correct amount, your company has refused to reinstate my card. In fact, the suspended card has now been canceled because of "possible fraudulent activity."

3 On September 2, I spoke to Mr. Ethan Adams, and I was led to believe that the problem would be resolved promptly. On September 4, when I still could not use the card, I spoke to Ms. Kira Russo. I was given to understand that I would have access to the card that very evening. However, when the card was not active on September 5, I called a third time and spoke to Mr. Sean McGee. [5]Notwithstanding the fact that I had been offered previous reassurances on two occasions, Mr. McGee informed me that the card had been canceled. When I asked to speak to a manager, I was connected to Ms. Hannah Cook, who insisted that company policy had been followed, and I would need to apply for a new card.

4 I understand that fraud is a legitimate concern, and I appreciate the need for online security. Nevertheless, however reasonable your policies may seem, I believe that good customer service takes into account the specific situation, in my case a simple human error. [6]I would have been happy to provide whatever form of identification was required.

5 I insist that my account be reactivated immediately. In fact, it is imperative that this issue be resolved by September 15 so that I can pay my college tuition. [7]In the event that I do not receive satisfaction, I will have no choice but to post the incident on Twitter and YouTube, as well as [8]consider legal action. I sincerely hope [9]these steps will not be necessary.

Thank you very much in advance for your assistance, and [10]I look forward to a response.

Sincerely yours,
Jacob Banks

Review 4
Units 7–8

1 Speaking

A Look at the photos on p.72.

1 Note down milestones for each phase of life using some of these expressions.

> act your age   come of age   come to terms with   conform to expectations   first-hand experience
> get off track   make it through   the stakes are higher   take charge   young at heart   wise beyond your years

2 In groups, share insights about what (you think) it's like to be each of the ages in the photos.

> By the time you're in your 30s, the stakes are a lot higher if you feel you've chosen the wrong profession. I've decided to find a new job."

> I'm not sure I agree. Even if you get off track, you're still young and can start over.

B Make it personal Do you believe in nature or nurture? Give examples of people you know about.

> I believe in nature. Haven't you read those studies of identical twins separated at birth who turn out to be exactly alike?

2 Grammar

A Rewrite the opinions (1–6) using cleft sentences.

1 Your age doesn't determine how creative you are. *It's not your age that determines how creative you are.*
2 The recession prevents many young people from getting jobs even if they've tried many times.
3 Having friends makes a difference when life gets tough even if your family is supportive.
4 Your parents made you the person you are now even if school is an influence.
5 Getting old doesn't cause depression; you can enjoy life at any age.
6 We have to face the challenge, though, even if we don't want to.

B Make it personal In pairs, share two true opinions from A.

> Given   In view of   So as to   With a view to   In an effort to   Thanks to   With the aim of

> It's your age that determines how creative you are. Young people have more ideas.

> I don't agree at all. My grandmother writes beautiful poetry.

C Complete the conversation with the verbs in parentheses in the future perfect (simple or continuous) form, or the subjunctive. (Some have more than one answer.)

Teacher: I suggest your son ¹_____ (try) to study harder before exams.
Parent: Yes, I wish he ²_____ (be) a better student. The problem is, he's on the soccer team and by the end of the year, he ³_____ (play) 50 games. He's never home.
Teacher: It's essential that he ⁴_____ (improve) his grades. If not, he won't get into college. He's already failed math twice.
Parent: I know. I'm really quite worried. Next year, he ⁵_____ (take) the same course for three years in a row.
Teacher: It was important that he ⁶_____ (study) for the exam last week, but I don't think he did.
Parent: I promise I'll talk to him when I get home.

D Rephrase the sentences in A. Use the adverb clauses of condition (1–6) at the beginning or end of the sentence.

1 *However* + adjective / adverb ...
2 *For all the* ...
3 *As much as* ...
4 *As useful as* ...
5 *Whatever* + noun ...
6 *As much as* ...

> However old you may be, it's not your age that determines how creative you are.

3 Reading

A Read the article on e-shopping. Note down five consumer problems and three actions you can take.

THE TRUTH ABOUT ONLINE SHOPPING

Nearly half of all online consumers have problems with online purchases, with issues ranging from unexpected fees to damaged merchandise. While there are more online customers than ever before, most never think about deliveries arriving late, not at all, or being left outside their homes without permission. Quality is hard to judge online, and some items may be better in a real store. Returning a purchase may require that you pay shipping charges. And finally, some consumers are victims of outright fraud. Many of them have no idea of their rights.

In the U.S., you have various options. Your state may have a Consumer Protection Office that can mediate complaints and conduct investigations. The Federal Trade Commission investigates fraud and offers useful tips for getting your money back. There's even an e-consumer government website to help you file complaints against international businesses. But most important, the Better Business Bureau helps you locate reputable businesses so you will not need these other services.

B **Make it personal** Using your notes in A, share a story about an e-purchase. Include the problem, what you've done until now, and what you plan to do to resolve it.

> For all the promises [name of business] may make, they never tell you about [type of problem]. When I bought ...

4 Self-test

Correct the two mistakes in each sentence. Check your answers in Units 7 and 8. What's your score, 1–20?

1 When I had children, my career came off track, something that was very hard to come to terms.
2 They say couples who have the same age get along best, but it's hard to meet people are my age.
3 When I'm old, I won't have been saving enough for retirement, but I will be working since my 20s.
4 My sister isn't the one who have problems because she's not the one who will have been taken care of our parents.
5 Would it be OK if I will apply for the job? I'm sure it will be a fascinating work.
6 We need to all take a stand about climate change and take legal action over companies that don't protect the environment.
7 It was important that you were not rude, but, unfortunately, you insisted that our manager not spoke at all.
8 I'm going to suggest her to go out of the way for our customers.
9 Notstanding the fact that I've written to the manager three times, it's been no avail.
10 By the time you open your new store, I will be coming here for 10 years and would really appreciate however discount you may be able to offer me.

5 Point of view

Choose a topic. Then support your opinion in 100–150 words, and record your answer. Ask a partner for feedback. How can you be more convincing?

a The 20s are the most important decade. OR
  Childhood is far more critical than your 20s.
b In 50 years, many social changes will have occurred. OR
  Change takes place slowly, and life won't have changed as much as people imagine.

9 Would you like to be a teacher?

1 Listening

A ▶9.1 Read the photo caption and guess the answer. Listen to the start of a radio show to check.

> Homeschooling is becoming [**more** / **less**] popular in the United States.

B ▶9.2 In groups, complete the chart. Then listen to the second part. How many of your ideas were mentioned?

Homeschooling	
What I (think I) know	What I'd like to know
It's popular in some European countries.	*Do parents prepare all the lessons?*

C ▶9.2 Listen again. Check (✔) the advantages mentioned. How many of your questions from **B** were answered?

Homeschooling …
1. ☐ enables students to do well academically later in life.
2. ☐ brings families closer together.
3. ☐ enables parents to cater to individual needs.
4. ☐ helps to avoid unnecessary interpersonal conflicts.
5. ☐ gives students more free time to pursue their own interests.

D ▶9.3 Listen to the third part. Circle the correct inferences.
Carlos feels that …
1. parents [**worry** / **don't worry enough**] about protecting their kids from outside influences.
2. [**not all** / **most**] parents have the natural aptitude to be good teachers.
3. both parents [**generally** / **don't always**] agree on whether to homeschool.
4. kids need to interact with [**only a few** / **all kinds of**] people to develop emotional intelligence.
5. homeschooling might make kids [**self-centered** / **lonely**].

E Make it personal Share your thoughts on homeschooling. Any big differences?
1. 🛜 Search on "homeschooling" to answer any remaining questions you have from **B**.
2. Which of the advantages / disadvantages in **C** and **D** are the most important? Can you add others?
3. Would you like to have been homeschooled? Would you ever homeschool your own children? Why (not)?

> On balance, I'm opposed to homeschooling, and it's not an option I'd choose for my kids.

> Really? But how can you be so sure?

♪ I can move to another town, Where nobody'd ask where you are now. LA or Mexico, No matter where I go, I can't outrun you

9.1

2 Vocabulary: Verbs beginning with *out*

A ▶9.4 Read *Out-* verbs. Then complete 1–4 with forms of the verbs in the mind map. Listen to check.

> **Out- verbs**
>
> The prefix *out-* in verbs usually means "better," "greater," "further," "longer," etc.
> He's a savvy politician who always manages to **outsmart** his rivals. (= be smarter than)
> In my neighborhood, houses **outnumber** apartments. (= There are more houses.)
> Adele **outsold** every female singer on the planet in the mid 2010s. (= sold more than)

1 Schools have stood the test of time and _____ countless societal changes and paradigm shifts.
2 Do the advantages of homeschooling _____ the potential drawbacks?
3 Apparently, homeschooled kids tend to _____ their public school peers on standardized tests to get into college.
4 We need to expose children to different people and environments to help them _____ their immaturity.

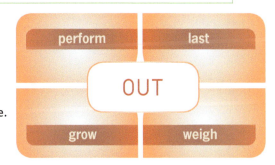

B Rephrase 1–4 using *out-* verbs. There may be more than one possible answer. Then ask and answer in pairs. Any disagreements?

1 Why are there more female than male teachers?
2 Is it a myth or fact that students who read widely tend to do better than those who don't?
3 When it comes to single-sex schools, are the pros greater than the cons?
4 On college campuses, why do PCs tend to sell more than tablets?

C Make it personal "Into" or "out of" the mainstream?

1 ▶9.5 **How to say it** Complete the chart. Listen to check.

Drawing tentative conclusions	
What they said	What they meant
1 It looks as _____ (it's crossing over into the mainstream).	It seems that ...
2 It would _____ that (the homeschool population is continuing to grow).	
3 This might have to _____ with the fact that (homeschooling offers both parents and children a great deal of flexibility).	Maybe this is related to ...
4 There might be some _____ to this.	Maybe this is true.

2 Read the headlines showing different educational trends in the United States. Which ones seem to be gaining popularity in your country, too? Note down some possible reasons.

1 Career-focused learning is back: High schools, community colleges, and companies push for a renewed emphasis on technical skills.

2 Not just for fun: Increasing evidence that music classes enhance performance in other subjects.

3 TAKING THE BULL BY THE HORNS: SCHOOLS RAMP UP ANTI-BULLYING EFFORTS

4 Size matters: Schools are packing more and more students into classrooms – and this is not a good

3 In pairs, compare your ideas. Use *out-* verbs and *How to say it* expressions. Similar opinions?

> Career-focused learning might have to do with the fact that these days, everyone needs to be an entrepreneur.

> Yes, new tech start-ups are beginning to outnumber traditional companies!

95

9.2 What is alternative medicine?

3 Language in use

A Read the excerpt from an article on acupuncture and answer 1–2.

1 The writer most likely thinks acupuncture …
   ☐ definitely works.   ☐ might work.   ☐ is ineffective.

2 In pairs, looking only at the cartoon …
   a summarize what acupuncture is.
   b list three conditions it might be used for.

ACUPUNCTURE

Acupuncture, the stimulation of points along the skin using thin needles, is thought to be effective for a variety of medical conditions. But it is really? Patients are reported to have been cured of pain, but some scientists say research is inconclusive, and it's unclear if this is a placebo effect. The technique is believed to relieve neck pain, migraines as well as less severe headaches, and lower back pain, and while many patients are thought to be helped, these scientists say more studies are needed. Of course, this is a Western point of view. In quite a few Asian countries, acupuncture is mainstream medicine, and in Mainland China, Japan, Hong Kong, and Taiwan, nearly everyone will tell you that acupuncture is known to have reduced patient suffering.

B Which view of acupuncture do you agree with? Is acupuncture popular where you live?

> I don't know if acupuncture is effective. I'd like to see more scientific evidence.

4 Pronunciation: Stress on three-word phrasal verbs

A ▶ 9.6 Complete the text with forms of the verbs in the box. Listen to a conversation between Emma and Luke to check. How many verbs did you know?

| come down with   give up on   go through with   grow out of   watch out for |

When Emma was a senior in high school, she ¹_____ (= began to suffer from) migraines at least once a week. Her mom thought she would ²_____ (= stop having) them, but she often missed school. The doctors couldn't help and Emma almost ³_____ (= stopped hoping for) a cure. Fortunately, though, her mom ⁴_____ (= was looking for) new treatments, and she discovered aromatherapy. Even though it didn't help right away, Emma decided to ⁵_____ the treatment (= finish it to the end).

B ▶ 9.7 Listen to the verbs in A and check (✔) the correct rule. Then repeat each one.

Three-word phrasal verbs are always stressed on the   ☐ first   ☐ second   ☐ third word.

C Make it personal In pairs, discuss 1–3. Include three-word phrasal verbs, where possible.

1 Have you ever tried acupuncture or aromatherapy? Would you like to?
2 Why might some people be opposed to alternative medicine?
3 Do you know anyone who's had a medical problem that wouldn't go away? Would either treatment have helped?

> My grandmother came down with the flu and developed asthma, but I don't think acupuncture would have helped …

♪ Say something, I'm giving up on you. I'm sorry that I couldn't get to you. Anywhere I would've followed you

9.2

5 Grammar: Passive expressions with infinitives

A Read the grammar box and check (✔) the correct rules (1–4).

Passive expressions in sentences with active and passive infinitives				
The treatment	is	reported	to	work well.
		thought		have helped.
Patients	are	known		be easily influenced.
		believed		have been cured.

1 The blue phrases are ☐ active ☐ passive. They refer to the ☐ present ☐ past.
2 The red phrase is ☐ active ☐ passive. It refers to the ☐ present ☐ past.
3 The green phrase is ☐ active ☐ passive, and the purple phrase is ☐ active ☐ passive.
4 The green and purple phrases describe events that ☐ happened in the past
   ☐ are happening right now.

» Grammar expansion p.154

B Find four more examples in 3A of passive expressions in sentences with infinitives. In pairs, say why each infinitive is like the red, green, blue, or purple example.

> The first one is "Acupuncture is thought to be effective": I think it's red. The infinitive is "to be" and it refers to the present. It's active because the subject is "acupuncture."

C Rewrite underlined sentences 1–6 from the forum to contain passive expressions and infinitives. Begin with the words in italics. How many infinitives are passive, too?

● **Eileen Finley, U.S.**
There are so many kinds of alternative medicine. ¹People think *homeotherapy* is helpful. It uses natural substances to treat infections, fatigue, allergies, and chronic illnesses like arthritis.

● **Héctor González, Mexico**
²Doctors believe biofeedback assists *patients*. By using techniques such as visualizing, relaxing, and imaging, it can treat asthma, migraines, insomnia, and high blood pressure.

● **Lester Silver, Canada**
How about Bach flower remedies, the system of herbal remedies developed by Edward Bach? ³Supporters report that they provide relief for personality problems and emotional issues. ⁴We know that they've cured *many* people.

● **Patricia Moreno, Colombia**
⁵We know that *Feng Shui* has helped some people, and I believe in it myself. It's an ancient Chinese practice where the furniture in a room is arranged and colors chosen to promote vital energy.

● **Betty Shih, Taiwan**
Don't forget hypnotherapy! Hypnosis bypasses the conscious mind and draws on suppressed memories to help with phobias, weight loss, and stress. ⁶People report that *it's* a miracle treatment!

D 🌐 **Make it personal** What are the best alternative treatments?

1 Choose two treatments from **C** or search on "types of alternative medicine" to find information about one of those below.

   dance therapy   fasting   massage therapy   Reiki   vitamin therapy   yoga therapy

2 Note down at least two reasons why they would be effective. For which ailments?
3 In groups, state your case. Use passive expressions with infinitives where possible.

> Dance therapy is reported to be helpful for physical disabilities and eating disorders.

> That may be, but it's also just fun and a great way to lose weight.

9.3 What unconventional families do you know?

6 Reading

A Read the first three paragraphs of the article. In pairs, list three possible advantages and three disadvantages of single parenting. Then read the rest. Were any of your ideas mentioned?

Four Reasons It's Better To Be A Single Parent
By Kerri Zane

Although the gold standard in child rearing has traditionally been a dual family unit, being a single parent has myriad benefits. Rather than navigating the treacherous territory of constant parental compromise, you can independently make choices for your children that you feel are best. Eleven years ago, when my former husband and I split, I saw my divorce as a glorious opportunity to parent solo. No more discussing the finer points of gymnastics vs. volleyball. I didn't have to debate dessert after dinner vs. never ever letting sugar touch lips. And there was no longer a lengthy discussion over the reason my daughters needed braces.

While the state of rock-steady marital bliss in the United States continues to falter, more and more adults are joining the ranks of contented uncoupled family units. In fact, based on the latest Census Bureau statistics, there are over 14 million single-parent households with children under the age of 18. That is a lot of people and a good reason to celebrate. Which is why March 21 has been designated as National Single Parents' Day. It is a time to honor all those tenacious individuals who do what they do, day in and day out, to support, nurture and care for their kids.

As the single mom expert and author of the Amazon best-selling book, *It Takes All 5: A Single Mom's Guide to Finding The REAL One*, I would like to honor the day and offer you four solid reasons why it's better to be a single mom or dad than half of a parenting pair.

1. No Negotiations Necessary
While your married counterparts continue to disagree on the state of their children's welfare, you get to make unilateral choices. In the long run this is better for your offspring's well-being. A child's behavior can be negatively affected by adult arguing. It will either leave them crying their eyes out or running for cover. With no one else in the house to challenge your choices, you may continue to be the cozy constant security blanket your children need. Granted, there is a financial price to pay when you are the sole provider, but children need to learn that sometimes we can't give them everything they want. And often times what they thought was a "must-have," really isn't. Ultimately, if it is that important, you will find a way. Payment plans are designed for the single parent!

2. Stellar Independent Role Model
One of the best gifts I was able to give my two daughters was the knowledge that they can make it on their own. Change a light bulb without a dad in the house — snap Mom. Swoop a stylish up-do for your teen with no mom in sight — yeah Dad. You embody the idea that it's better to "want" to be in a relationship because there is a loving bond, rather than you "need" to be in a relationship because there is stuff to be done or procured. When your child sees you as a completely whole and independent adult, they will learn to emulate your healthy behaviors.

3. Relationship Options May Vary
Our society is shifting away from the bonds of matrimony. A recent Pew study revealed that just over half of adult Americans are married, the lowest rate in decades. Children will be enlightened and possibly relieved that they are no longer tied to that traditional lifestyle. Marriage is optional and sometimes not applicable. Long-term relationships without wedding bands can be stronger. My idols in this arena are Kurt Russell and Goldie Hawn; they've been together for nearly 30 years. These lessons are particularly important for girls, who've been raised on the fictitious belief that Prince Charming would sweep them off their feet to live happily ever after. There is a real possibility that they can become enormously disappointed when their fairytale ending turns into a hardcore courtroom reality.

🎵 I'm a survivor. I'm not gonna give up. I'm not gonna stop. I'm gonna work harder

4. Building a Better Body

Marriages are like your freshman year in college. You have the tendency to pack on the pounds. One study found that women could gain five to eight pounds in the first few years of their wedded bliss and a whopping 54 pounds by the ten-year anniversary mark. Their single counterparts stay slim. Most of us have an **overriding desire** to want to be attractive to **prospective mates** of the opposite sex. The result of a divorce? A slimmer, trimmer you — aka the Divorce Diet. Take a look at Tom Cruise who reportedly lost 15 pounds after splitting with Katie. Jennie Garth lost 20 and Demi Moore has been stick thin since the departure of her sweetheart, Ashton Kutcher.

Many reports will tell you that being a single parent is stressful. It is. But no more stressful than being a married parent. Ultimately, we all want to step into our own with confidence and take every curveball life throws us with our independent spirit intact. The best way to handle the inevitable life shifts is to stay positive, reach out for support from your friends and family, relish the time you spend with your children and most importantly, create a daily space for some much deserved me-time.

Happy National Single Parents' Day to you!

B Statements 1–6 are true, according to the author. Underline the evidence in the article.
1 Children benefit when only one parent makes all decisions.
2 Single-parenting can be financially challenging.
3 Relationships should be based on love rather than mutual dependence.
4 Women grow up believing that they're destined to find the perfect partner.
5 People tend to put on weight in marriage, just like when they start college.
6 Optimism and meaningful relationships can help you cope with life's changes.

C ▶9.8 Read *Common collocations and compounds*. Then listen to and re-read the article focusing on the highlighted phrases. In pairs, use context to work out what they mean.

Common collocations and compounds

Adjective–noun collocations and compound nouns are common, but distinguishing common expressions from an author's personal style can be hard. Memorize expressions you see frequently.

	Common	Writer's style
collocations	fictitious belief, overriding desire, prospective mate, lengthy discussion, unilateral choices	parental compromise, tenacious individuals
compound nouns	child rearing, fairytale ending, security blanket	parenting pair, divorce diet, life shifts

> A "fictitious belief" is obviously a belief that is false. I don't believe in Prince Charming!

D Make it personal In pairs, react to the author's article. Discuss 1–3. Use common collocations and compounds. Do you both agree?
1 How balanced is her presentation of single parenting?
2 How many of your points in **A** were mentioned? Which are most important?
3 Which statements in **B** do you agree with? Why (not)?

> I don't agree with number 1. A good partner helps in decision-making and provides you with a security blanket, too.

> But what about Kerri Zane's arguments? Don't you agree that …?

» 9.4 How often do you work out?

7 Language in use

A ▶9.9 Match a–e to the photos. Then listen to conversations 1–5 and match them to the photos.

| a a treadmill   b stretching   c weightlifting   d sit-ups   e abs |

A   B   C   D   E

B ▶9.10 In pairs, take the quiz. Listen to a personal trainer to check. Any surprises?

Test your fitness IQ!	A fact	Hmm … Not so simple!
1 Running on a treadmill will protect your knees.		
2 Calorie counters in fitness machines are usually accurate.		
3 You don't need to sweat to burn calories.		
4 Stretching before weightlifting prevents injury.		
5 If you do lots of sit-ups, you'll get toned abs.		

C ▶9.11 Read *Verbs ending in -en*. Then complete 1–5 with verbs formed from words in the box. Listen to check.

> **Verbs ending in -en**
>
> The *-en* suffix can be used to make verbs from adjectives or nouns.
> 1 Light and color: *I'm going to have my teeth **whitened** (adj: white) tomorrow.*
> 2 Size, density, and movement: *Don't **lengthen** (n: length) your workout beyond your level of endurance and **lessen** (adj: less) your expectations for quick progress.*
> 3 Others: *Things have **worsened** (adj: worse) and his neighbor has **threatened** (n: threat) him.*

| bright   fresh   soft   strength   weak |

1 Most treadmills include padding that can stop your knees from hurting because, just like a cushion, it _____ any impact you may feel, unlike a hard surface outdoors.
2 Some machines can overestimate calorie count by over 40%! These numbers might put a smile on your face and _____ your day, but don't let them fool you! You can't count on them being right!
3 Sweating keeps you from overheating – and having to stop to _____ up every five minutes! But rest assured that you can burn hundreds of calories without necessarily dripping in sweat.
4 Some studies show that stretching before weightlifting won't necessarily enable you to perform better and might actually _____ your muscles!
5 Toning exercises will help you _____ your abs, but may not give you a really flat tummy.

D 🌐 **Make it personal** Search on "fitness myths" and find at least one more to share in groups. Whose was the most surprising?

> Here's one to brighten your day! Working out actually lessens your craving for food!

100

♪ Something in the way you move, Makes me feel like I can't live without you. It takes me all the way. I want you to stay

9.4

8 Grammar: Overview of verb patterns

A Read the grammar box and write a–d in the white boxes for patterns 1–4. Then choose an underlined verb from **7C** for each example.

	Verb patterns with adjectives, gerunds, base forms, and infinitives			
a	My coach	**makes**	me	**stay** focused.
b	Exercise	**encourages**	people	**to socialize**.
		will **cause**	your blood pressure	**to drop**.
c	Parents	should **discourage**	young kids	**from overexercising**.
d	I	really **appreciate**	your	**helping** me.

verb + object + …

1 ☐ infinitive (e.g., _____)
2 ☐ base form (e.g., _____)
3 ☐ -ing form (e.g., _____)
4 ☐ preposition + -ing form (e.g., _____)

» Grammar expansion p.154

B ▶ 9.12 Circle the correct answer. Listen, check, and write a–d next to each underlined verb.
1 Maybe you won't <u>dissuade</u> ☐ me [**from giving** / **to give**] it a shot then.
2 I <u>urge</u> ☐ [**that you see** / **you to see**] your doctor before you begin exercising.
3 <u>Have</u> ☐ your doctor [**help** / **helping**] you choose the best exercise program for you.
4 Sweat is a sign that your body is <u>reminding</u> ☐ itself [**to cool** / **of cooling**] down.
5 My doctor <u>warned</u> ☐ me not [**to stretch** / **stretch**] before weightlifting.
6 I won't <u>insist on</u> ☐ your [**listen** / **listening**] to me instead.

Common mistake
Can you help me *choose* ~~choosing~~ a good gym?

C Rephrase 1–7. Use the correct form of the verbs in parentheses and begin with the underlined words.

Fact or myth?

1 You can lose weight faster by taking <u>cold showers</u>. (help)
2 Take <u>large doses</u> of vitamin C and you won't get the flu. (stop)
3 Teens no longer develop social skills because of <u>cell phones</u>. (prevent)
4 People still use their cars even if there are <u>bike lanes</u> available. (not dissuade)
5 Students remember information better when <u>taking notes by hand</u>. (enable)
6 <u>Violent video games</u> make children behave aggressively. (encourage)
7 Compared to maps, <u>a GPS</u> makes it easier for you to find your location. (let)

Let's check!

D **Make it personal** Fact or myth? In groups, do 1–2.
1 Individually, choose three statements from **C**. Write M (myth) or F (fact) next to each one.
2 In groups, support your opinion. Use verb patterns from **A**. Who's most convincing?

Cold showers really help people lose weight! They make your metabolism work faster.

I've heard that, too. I went on a "cold-shower diet" once, but I gave up after a month!

9.5 What are the pros and cons of dieting?

9 Listening

A ▶9.13 Use the photo to guess what a raw vegan diet includes. Listen to Terri and Hugo and cross out the foods that don't belong.

B ▶9.13 Listen again. Terri most likely ...
- [ ] thinks Hugo has made a good decision.
- [ ] considers the diet a bit weird.
- [ ] is firmly opposed to Hugo's choice.

C ▶9.14 Listen to the rest. T (true), F (false), or NI (no information)? Correct the false statements.
1. A raw vegan diet contains no carbohydrates.
2. Carbohydrates aren't found in fruit.
3. A salad is a better protein source than fruit.
4. Adults usually find the diet easy to get used to.
5. Lack of vitamin D can have dangerous consequences in children.

D Make it personal In pairs, would you like to try a raw vegan diet? Support your opinion with at least three reasons.

> I think it would be very hard to find places to eat.

> Not any longer. There are lots of "raw" restaurants these days.

10 Keep talking

A ▶9.15 **How to say it** Complete the chart. Listen to Terri's responses to check.

Reacting to new information	
What they said	What they meant
1 I should _____ judgment.	I should be more open minded.
2 Did I hear you _____?	You must be joking.
3 Who in their _____ mind (would eat so many bananas)?	You'd have to be crazy (to eat so many bananas).
4 _____, but no thanks!	No way!

B In groups, report on out-of-the-mainstream choices!

1. 🌐 Search for an article online on a topic below. Is it basically pro or con? Note down the main arguments.

FOUR WAYS TO GET OUT OF THE MAINSTREAM!

1. Quit your high-stress, high-paying job now! Be a "taxi" tour guide or dog walker, instead.
2. Repelled by an image-conscious society? Support a ban on plastic surgery ads.
3. Let your children be "free to roam." Reject structured after-school activities.
4. Become "technology free." Throw out your cell phone and delete your Facebook profile.

2. Would you personally consider this choice? Support your "decision" with information you've found. Use *How to say it* expressions where possible.

> An article called [name] says being a "taxi" tour guide pays well.

> I should reserve judgment, but is that safe?

♪ I am beautiful no matter what they say. Words can't bring me down. I am beautiful in every single way

9.5

11 Writing: A report on pros and cons

A Read the report on the pros and cons of homeschooling. It can be inferred that the writer …
  a ☐ is for homeschooling.
  b ☐ is against homeschooling.
  c ☐ wants parents to make their own decisions.

Extensive research has been done on homeschooling, a growing trend in the United States and many other countries. Nevertheless, it is unclear whether observed benefits are actually caused by homeschooling, as opposed to other factors. For that reason, the decision to homeschool continues to be a very personal one. My neighbors struggled with this decision.

1 Among the many reasons given for homeschooling are the ability to …
  • customize the curriculum and offer more individual attention.
  • experiment with pedagogical methods different from those used in schools.
  • enhance family relationships.
  • provide a safe environment for learners.
  • impart a particular set of values and beliefs.

2 It is claimed that students who are homeschooled …
  • outperform their peers on achievement tests, regardless of parents' income or level of formal education.
  • do above average on measures of social and psychological development.
  • succeed at college at a higher rate than the general population, are more tolerant, and are more involved in community service.

3 Nevertheless, potential arguments against homeschooling are just as numerous.
  • Time: Organizing lessons, teaching, giving tests, and planning field trips are labor-intensive activities.
  • Cost: Buying the newest teaching tools, computer equipment, and books can eat into the family budget.
  • Effort: Ensuring adequate opportunities for socialization with other children, including those from other countries and backgrounds, calls for careful planning.
  • Patience: Separating the roles of parent and teacher requires a calm attitude.

I was homeschooled and it wasn't for me. Every child is a unique individual, as is every parent who homeschools. A child's needs and how optimum learning can be achieved remain the overriding concerns.

B Read the *Guidelines for good reports*. Then cross out two personal sentences in the report in **A** that don't belong.

Guidelines for good reports

A good report on a topic …
• has a clear thesis and conclusion.
• is short and succinct.
• keeps the reader interested by avoiding repetition: different verbs or nouns start each point.
• does not include irrelevant personal information or opinions.

C Read *Write it right!* Then find the section that …
  a ☐ has items beginning with nouns.
  b ☐ has ones with verbs.
  c ☐ contains nouns with -*ing* forms.

Write it right!

For lists in reports, begin each item in a section with a similar style. For example, in section 1, all points begin with infinitives.
Homeschooling offers the ability **to** …
• customize the curriculum.
• experiment with different methods.
Sections don't all need to be identical, just consistent. They may also begin with nouns or verbs.

D Rewrite the list with a consistent style. There may be more than one solution.

If you are considering homeschooling …
  • it's important to take into account the time involved.
  • set aside money for materials.
  • finding possible friends for your children is important, too.
  • you should always be patient in your "home classroom."

E Your turn! Choose a topic that you discussed in **10B** and write a report in about 280 words that includes two to three lists.

Before
Plan the main function of each list. Note down specific information for three to five bullet points. Search online for more details if necessary.

While
Write three to four sections, following the model in **A**. Include a clear thesis and conclusion, and refer to *Write it right!* for style.

After
Post your report online and read your classmates' work. Give suggestions for clarity and consistency.

10

Why do friends drift apart?

1 Listening

A ▶10.1 Listen to Henry reminiscing about his college years. How close is he to his old friends? Why?

B ▶10.2 Listen to the second part. Label Mike (M) and Bruce (B) in the pictures. There's one extra.

C ▶10.2 Match 1–4 with the topics a–d. Listen to check. Do you understand the expressions in context?

1 "The writing was on the wall."
2 "What a riot he was!"
3 "Whatever became of him?"
4 "Go figure."

a ☐ Henry's sister wonders what Bruce is doing.
b ☐ Henry was surprised by Bruce.
c ☐ Bruce was different from Mike.
d ☐ Henry and Mike didn't have much in common.

D ▶10.3 Listen to the last part. In pairs, explain 1–2. Will Henry follow the advice? Why (not)?

1 what Henry meant by "abducted by aliens"
2 Henry's sister's advice, "Don't judge a book by its cover"

> He might mean / be suggesting ...

E Make it personal Do opposites attract?

1 ▶10.4 **How to say it** Complete the chart with a form of *say* or *tell*. Listen to check.

Clarifying: Expressions with *say* and *tell*	
What they said	What they meant
1 I guess it goes without _____ (that) ...	It must be obvious that ...
2 Truth be _____ , ...	Honestly, ...
3 There's no _____ why, but ...	It's hard to explain why, but ...
4 _____ what you will ...	You might have your reservations ...
5 Easier _____ than done!	That's easy to suggest, but hard to put into practice!

2 Note down answers to a–c. In pairs, tell each other about someone you see often, but who's very different from you. Use *How to say it* expressions.

a Who's the person? Are you in close touch with him / her out of choice or obligation?
b Do your differences bother you, or have they strengthened your relationship. In what way?
c Have you ever fallen out temporarily? What happened?

> My friend María is my polar opposite. There's no telling why we're friends!

> So are you saying you don't enjoy her company?

If you wanna be my lover, You gotta get with my friends. Make it last forever, Friendship never ends

2 Vocabulary: Friendship idioms

A ▶ 10.5 Match each question or comment (1–6) to its reply (a–f). Listen to check.

1 The three of you were inseparable!
2 Bruce was the exact opposite, always the life of the party.
3 Our conversations never went beneath the surface.
4 You guys go back a long way, right?
5 Do you still see her?
6 OK, so you don't see eye to eye on everything. So what?

a ☐ Yeah, all you could talk about was soccer and video games.
b ☐ No, she was a breath of fresh air, though.
c ☐ We do! We went to high school together.
d ☐ Yes, what a riot he was!
e ☐ But it's important to agree on things, isn't it?
f ☐ Yes, we were birds of a feather.

B Rephrase underlined sentences 1–6 using highlighted expressions from **A**. Use the correct tense. Then choose two expressions to describe someone you know.

Five types of friends you need to have in your life. Who are yours?
INTERESTING CATEGORIES. HERE'S MY LIST. — Louise762

1 THE HONEST CONFIDANT: GUY
¹He's a welcome change. He's still the one I turn to when I need to hear the truth, and nothing but the truth.

2 THE SOUL MATE: LORNA
²Lorna and I are very similar in character. She's a terrific listener, and when we're having a serious conversation, ³she can see beyond the obvious and have insights that none of my other friends can.

3 THE POLAR OPPOSITE: JULIA
It's funny how Julia and I have become friends even though ⁴we don't seem to agree on anything. But, honestly, why would I want to surround myself with people just like me?

4 A FRIENDLY NEIGHBOR: RON
Ron moved to the neighborhood in 2005, so ⁵we've known each other for ages! He's really helpful and dependable, and above all, a good listener.

5 A WORK PAL: HUGO
In an office full of boring people, Hugo is a breath of fresh air. ⁶He makes me laugh! ⁷He's a lot of fun! He's always telling jokes, even when we're stressed out.

> My next-door neighbor is a breath of fresh air. He's always in a good mood!

C Make it personal What's the nature of friendship?

1 In groups, explain what the quotes below mean to you.

1 "The best mirror is an old friend." (George Herbert)
2 "A friend to all is a friend to none." (Aristotle)
3 "And like a favorite old movie, sometimes the sameness in a friend is what you like the most about her." (Emily Giffin)
4 "I would rather walk with a friend in the dark than alone in the light." (Helen Keller)
5 "In prosperity our friends know us; in adversity we know our friends." (John Churton Collins)
6 "You will evolve past certain people. Let yourself." (Mandy Hale)

> The first one must mean, "An old friend sees you as you really are and reflects that back."

> But do you agree? Don't friends sometimes see someone like themselves?

2 Vote on your three favorites. Why do they resonate?

10.2 Who's the oldest person you know?

3 Language in use

A ▶10.6 Listen to the start of a lecture. Which factor may be most important for longevity, according to the speaker? Which two photos (1–3) are her Aunt Agatha?

1

2

3

B ▶10.7 Listen to the rest of the lecture and complete the slide. Any surprises?

> **THE KEY TO LONGEVITY**
>
> - Regular ¹_____ _____ is just as important as diet and ²_____.
> - ³_____ _____ can be much more harmful than ⁴_____.
> - The size of our ⁵_____ _____ is slightly more important than the ⁶_____ of our ⁷_____ – but only during ⁸_____ and old age.
> - In other words: The more ⁹_____ your ¹⁰_____ are, the ¹¹_____ and ¹²_____ your life may be.

C ▶10.8 Read *To as a preposition*. Then correct the mistakes, if any, in 1–5. Listen to check.

> **To as a preposition**
>
> If *to* is followed by the base form of a verb, it's part of an infinitive:
> I wouldn't **want to live** to a hundred if that means having a boring, overly healthy lifestyle.
>
> If it's followed by the *-ing* form, it's a preposition:
> I can understand why people **look forward to retiring**. There's more to life than just working.
>
> It's easy to know which is which. Try putting a noun after *to*. If you can, it's a preposition:
> I know I should **limit myself to (having) two cups** of coffee a day, but I can't!

1 What's the secret to living a long and healthy life?
2 Let me try to answer this question by way of a personal anecdote.
3 She came close to win a marathon.
4 Aunt Agatha managed to track down some of her school friends.
5 Social connections might be the key to have good overall health.

D **Make it personal** In groups, discuss 1–2. Similar opinions?

1 Re-read the sentences in the box in **C**. Modify them so they're true for you.
2 Which potential risks would you give up?

delicious, but fatty food   fun, but potentially dangerous sports
travel by plane, car, or motorcycle   weekend parties, but not enough sleep
a well-paid, but totally sedentary job

> The key to living longer is having a good time, so I'm never giving up parties.

♪ It's my life. It's now or never. I ain't gonna live forever. I just want to live while I'm alive

10.2

4 Grammar: Degrees of comparison

A Read the grammar box. Then put sentences 1–7 in the categories below.

Degrees of comparison with *the ... the*, *more / ... er*, and *as ... as*				
1 **The** more friends	you have,	**the** happier	you'll feel.
2 **The** healthier	your diet (is),	**the** longer	you'll live.
3 I'm	much / far / a (whole) lot	clos**er** to my sister **than** (to)	my mom.
4 She's	a little / a bit / slightly	**more** traditional **than**	we are. us.
5 Friends are	every bit / just	**as** important **as**	family.
6 Family is	nowhere near		friends.
7 Friends are**n't**	quite	**as** close **as**	family.

» Grammar expansion p.156

Parallel or equal meaning	Big difference of degree	Small difference of degree

B Check (✔) the sentence(s) that mean(s) the same as the four points in **3B**.
1 ☐ Regular social contact is every bit as important as diet and exercise.
2 ☐ Social isolation is nowhere near as harmful as obesity.
3 ☐ For a small part of our lives, the size of our social network isn't quite as important as the quality of our friendships.
4 ☐ Meaningful relationships have a big impact on your health and lifespan.

C Rephrase the underlined sentences using the words in the box. Keep the same meaning.

1 The older   2 nowhere near   3 not quite   4 a whole lot   5 slightly   6 every bit

Marriage in later life

- ¹When you're older, you're more dependent on other people, and for many, this means one's husband or wife. So to what extent does marriage improve life expectancy?
- Marriage has traditionally been a non-biological factor that correlates positively with life expectancy. For one thing, ²married people take risks far less often than single people. Marriage also gives you more social and economic support.
- However, ³the health differences between married and single people are slightly less significant than they used to be. This may be because people are committing to each other in different ways.
- ⁴Research also shows that people who are single, especially men, are living much longer lives than ever before. It would appear that they are taking more responsibility for their own health and well-being.
- ⁵Widows and widowers aren't quite as healthy as people who are married. No one really knows exactly why. Maybe married people can count on an extended family to help them out. Besides, the widowed are more likely to be isolated, and ⁶social isolation can be very bad for your health.

D **Make it personal** In groups, discuss 1–3. Any interesting ideas?
1 Were you aware of the research in **3B**? Is it convincing? Why (not)?
2 Does being married help with social integration where you live?
3 In what ways might being married actually shorten some people's lives?

Common mistake
the sooner you'll finish
The sooner you start, ~~you will finish sooner~~.

Well, the less fulfilling your relationship is, the shorter your life might be! Doesn't stress shorten life?

That could be, but you don't have to stay in an unhappy marriage.

107

10.3 How easy is it to make friends where you live?

5 Reading

A In pairs, guess the author's answer to the article question. To what extent can nationality predict human behavior?

B ▶ 10.9 Read and listen to the article. Check (✔) all that apply. Does the author seem to agree with your answers in A?

The author compares Germans and Americans in _____ terms.

1 ☐ social 2 ☐ economic 3 ☐ historical 4 ☐ gender-related

Are American Friendships Superficial?

Why do many immigrants consider American friendships superficial?

1 I was speaking to a German woman who has lived in the United States for a decade and has made it her permanent home. She was describing her likes and dislikes about the U.S. in comparison to Germany. For example, on the positive side, she was enthusiastic about the opportunities for work and advancement she had found here based on her skills and accomplishments – as opposed to Germany, where an insistence on the right credentials is often insurmountable. On the negative side, however, she complained that American friendships are superficial.

2 I have heard this criticism before, with variations – "no deep friendships," "people form and dissolve relationships too easily," "you don't know if you can really trust people," and so forth.

3 She also described a misunderstanding with a co-worker, who referred to her as a friend. "You're not my friend," she said. "You're an acquaintance. We go out for coffee together and chat about things. That's not friendship." The woman was offended – not surprisingly. Telling someone in the U.S. "You're not my friend," is tantamount to saying "You're my enemy." It took quite a while for her to overcome this misstep.

What is going on here?

4 To begin with, in a conversation Germans tend to be quite direct. (An American might joke that their words are so long that there is no time left to beat around the bush.) Where an American might say "From my point of view, I see it this way," a German might simply say, "I think X." Direct speech can seem inconsiderate to Americans. In this regard, Brazilians are to Americans as Americans are to Germans. Americans who are new to Brazil complain that "You never know what Brazilians think." or even "People are always lying to me." From the Brazilian point of view, they're being considerate, modulating what they say according to the non-verbal reactions of the other person, so as to have an agreeable conversation.

5 Germany is also part of the Old World. A family may live in the same town, or even the same house, for several centuries; everyone knows everyone, and personal relationships develop gradually over extended periods of time. The United States has only been around for two centuries. We are a nation of immigrants, and time begins for many families with their arrival here. Our history of wagon trains and the conquest of the West involved a similar internal migration experience – breaking the ties of family and friendship, and then forming new ones.

6 American individualism means that we give more emphasis to our own needs in forming and dissolving relationships than do cultures organized around traditional forms and relationships. This means that people who don't know one another can form groups to satisfy common needs. In criticizing what she viewed as the superficiality of our friendships, the German woman also praised the existence of numerous informal groups – around hobbies, interests, work, self-improvement, religion, and so forth – that make it possible to meet new people.

7 For generations, America has been the world center of capitalism; and capitalism prizes a mobile labor force. Thus, it is not surprising that many Americans have developed the ability to form and dissolve relationships, as they are periodically uprooted to earn a living or advance a career in another city, state, or region.

8 I should also mention that, during her childhood, the place where the woman grew up was in East Germany. Before reunification, the Stasi (secret police) were an omnipresent danger. People never knew, if they told someone their true thoughts and feelings, whether the information could be passed on to be used against them. Trusting someone as a friend could mean putting your life in their hands – a much greater commitment than friendship here. Even though that time has passed, the more intense commitment involved in friendship lingers on.

9 German-English dictionaries define friend as *Freund* and vice versa. But clearly, despite many features in common, the two words are not equivalent. Friendship in the United States and Germany is similar but not the same. As I told the woman about her co-worker, "She was your friend, but not your *Freundin*."

♪ You won't ever find him being unfaithful. You will find him, You'll find him next to me

10.3

C Re-read the article. Circle words or phrases that show the woman's views on friendship in Germany. Underline those for the United States.

D Scan the article and find …
1 an expression that means "equivalent to": _____ (paragraph 3)
2 an idiom that means the *opposite* of "get straight to the point": _____ (paragraph 4)
3 an adjective that means "pleasant": _____ (paragraph 4)
4 a verb that means "remains, but is gradually disappearing": _____ (paragraph 8)

E Make it personal Friendships across cultures. In groups, discuss 1–2.
1 When it comes to making friends, is your country more like Germany or the United States?
2 Do you have any friends from other cultures? To what extent have they challenged your views on …?

> the relative importance of family
> socializing and dating
> gender roles
> money

> Here in [name of country], we would never tell anyone "You're not my friend." I think we're more like the U.S.

6 Vocabulary: Words with both prefixes and suffixes

A Read *Double affixation*. Then write the root words (1–7) as they are spelled in isolation. Were any letters dropped or changed?

> **Double affixation**
>
> Many adjectives, nouns, and adverbs are made up of a **prefix**, a **root word**, and a **suffix**:
> In Germany, an insistence on the right credentials is often **insurmountable**.
> Here, *in-* means "not," *surmount* means "overcome," and *-able* means "that can be."
> " So, *insurmountable* means "that can't be overcome." Remember: spelling sometimes changes, too.
> I was shocked by their **unfriendliness**. (un + friendly + ness)

1 discouraging   3 interdependence   5 counterproductive   7 impolitely
2 ineffective   4 unreliable   6 misunderstanding

B ▶ 10.10 Match the three columns to find six words. Then write the full words with the correct spelling. Listen to two conversations about stereotypes to check.

Prefix		Root word				Suffix	
dis	in	1	mature	4	resist	able	ible
il	ir	2	taste	5	logic	al	ive
im	un	3	accept	6	expense	ful	ity

C ▶ 10.10 Listen again. Summarize each stereotype in one sentence. Any truth to them?

D Make it personal Complete 1–5 with popular stereotypes where you live. In groups, compare your ideas. Which ones are most common?

1 _____ are bad drivers.
2 _____ can be a bit rude.
3 _____ tend to be lazy.
4 _____ is a dangerous place.
5 _____ (You choose!)

> Here in [name of city], [neighborhood] is really dangerous.

> That's just a stereotype! I live there, and I've never had any problems.

109

10.4 Have you ever met someone new by chance?

7 Language in use

A ▶10.11 Listen to the start of a radio show. Choose the correct answer.

> "Six Degrees of Separation" means we're [further away / closer] to people than we think.

B ▶10.12 Look at the pictures on the right and read the conversation excerpts. Listen to the next part. Check (✔) the callers that believe the "Six Degrees of Separation" theory.

C ▶10.12 Listen again and note down key details. In pairs, summarize each story.

> So in the first one, this guy was in a bad mood and went out to eat ...

D ▶10.13 Read *Expressions with odds*. Then listen and match excerpts 1–5 with the correct pattern (a–e). Continue listening to check.

> **Expressions with *odds***
>
> The word *odds*, meaning "chances" is very common in English and takes various patterns.
> The odds **of** see**ing** him were **50 to 1**.
> What are **the odds that** I could get that job?

a ☐ the odds of [object] [verb]-*ing* ...
b ☐ the odds of [verb]-*ing* ...
c ☐ The odds are against you ...
d ☐ the odds that ...
e ☐ the odds are [number] to [number] that ...

E Make it personal In groups, use only the pictures from **B** and your notes from **C**, to decide which story is most surprising. Do you know of any similar experiences? Use expressions with *odds*.

> Number 5 is the most surprising. What are the odds of falling in love with a place that quickly?

> I think it's possible if you were looking to make a change in your life.

1 Had Sarah not come by with Tom, I wouldn't be married to her now! ☐

2 Should you need anything at all while Beth is away, just come by. You know I don't mind. ☐

3 Were I to have dialed a different phone number, my whole life would have been different! ☐

4 Had I called even a minute later, I might not have arrived in time. Eric saved my life! ☐

5 Were we to spend even one more day here, I'd never be able to leave. This is the most beautiful view I've ever seen. ☐

♪ I lost a friend, Somewhere along in the bitterness. And I would have stayed up with you all night, Had I known how to save a life

10.4

8 Grammar: Inverted conditional sentences

A Read the grammar box and choose the correct meaning below (a or b) for 1–5.

Inverted conditional sentences for present, past, or future time		
Were	**we to apologize**[1],	we could resume our friendship with Richard.
	I to have gone[2] home,	we never would have met.
Should	**you wish to come**[3] today,	just give us a call.
Had	**he contacted**[4] me on Facebook,	we could have seen each other.
	she not gone[5] to the party,	we wouldn't be married today.

Inverted conditional clauses can be used instead of *if*-clauses and sometimes add emphasis. They tend to be slightly more formal. *Had* is not contracted, and past sentences like *Were I to have gone ...* mean the same as *Had I gone ...*

» Grammar expansion p.156

1 a ☐ If we apologized   b ☐ If we had apologized
2 a ☐ If I went home   b ☐ If I'd gone home
3 a ☐ If you want to come today b ☐ If you came today
4 a ☐ If he'd contacted me on Facebook b ☐ If he contacted me on Facebook
5 a ☐ If she'd gone to the party b ☐ If she hadn't gone to the party

Common mistake
Had you not
~~Hadn't you~~ called, I would have worried.

B Underline the five inverted conditional sentences in **7B**. Which sentence(s) with a form of *be* can be reworded with a form of *have*?

C Rephrase the underlined clauses 1–6 in the forum entries. Use inverted conditional sentences and a form of the verbs in parentheses.

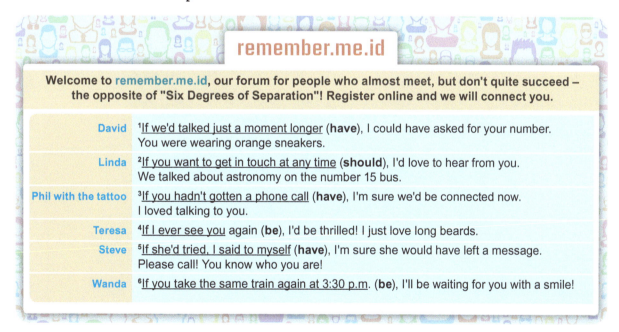

remember.me.id

Welcome to **remember.me.id**, our forum for people who almost meet, but don't quite succeed – the opposite of "Six Degrees of Separation"! Register online and we will connect you.

David — [1]If we'd talked just a moment longer (**have**), I could have asked for your number. You were wearing orange sneakers.

Linda — [2]If you want to get in touch at any time (**should**), I'd love to hear from you. We talked about astronomy on the number 15 bus.

Phil with the tattoo — [3]If you hadn't gotten a phone call (**have**), I'm sure we'd be connected now. I loved talking to you.

Teresa — [4]If I ever see you again (**be**), I'd be thrilled! I just love long beards.

Steve — [5]If she'd tried, I said to myself (**have**), I'm sure she would have left a message. Please call! You know who you are!

Wanda — [6]If you take the same train again at 3:30 p.m. (**be**), I'll be waiting for you with a smile!

D Make it personal Have you ever had an important "missed connection"? In groups, share a true or invented story. Whose is most surprising?

1 When / Where / Why / What / Who? Note down a few details.
2 What would have happened had you been able to connect?
3 If you could go back in time, what would you have done differently?
4 Were you to meet this person again, what would you do?

> When I was on the train last week, I saw an old girlfriend out of the corner of my eye. Had I reacted even one second sooner, I could have spoken to her!

10.5 How persuasive are you?

9 Listening

A In pairs, imagine you want to persuade a slightly antisocial friend to come to a party you're giving. What strategies would you use?

> I might say, "I've only invited people you know."

B ⏺ ▶ 10.14 Listen to / watch the first part of a video on persuasion (0:00–3:05). What do the party invitation and restaurant tipping have in common?

C ⏺ ▶ 10.14 Listen / Watch the first part again. Which statements do the speakers believe? Write Y (yes) or N (no). Correct the wrong ones.
1. Integrity is important when trying to persuade others.
2. Social plans don't involve obligation.
3. It's not only the size of a gift that counts, but also how the recipient feels.
4. Pleasant surprises make a strong impression.
5. It's usually not noticed when gifts are personalized.

D Make it personal In pairs, which statements in C do you agree with? Support your opinion with a personal story.

> I definitely agree with number 1. I'll never forget the time that ...

E ⏺ ▶ 10.15 Listen to / watch the "persuasion of liking" from 7:40 to 9:05. How did liking potato chips help the business students persuade others?

F ⏺ ▶ 10.15 In pairs, can you recall why we like people? Complete the notes. Then listen to / watch the second part again to check.

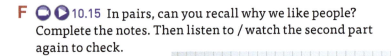

10 Keep talking

A Choose two questions and note down at least three points for each.
1. How can we persuade our parents, teachers, or boss to give us more independence?
2. Why is it difficult, but important, to sometimes say "no," even to those we like?
3. How have you been influenced by friends / family? Did they use strategies from 9E?

B Share opinions in groups, using these expressions. Any interesting stories or ideas?

They're far more likely to ... if ...	They persuaded me to ...
I'm nowhere near as ... by ... as ...	The more they ... , the more I ...

> I got to know my friend Victoria when she cooperated with me on a project. The closer I got to her, the more she influenced me ...

♪ Just say yes, just say there's nothing holding you back. It's not a test, nor a trick of the mind, Only love

10.5

11 Writing: A persuasive essay

A A persuasive opinion essay has a clear topic sentence, which may state subtopics to be developed in separate paragraphs. Read paragraph 1. What is the topic sentence?

B Read the rest. Then find three sentences in paragraphs 4, 5, and 6 that state each subtopic.

C Read *Write it right!* and write the strategy number (1, 2, or 3) next to the words in the box. Then complete 1–9 in the essay with an appropriate item.

Write it right!

A good persuasive essay appeals to the reader's feelings, and logically builds a persuasive argument. To do so, the writer uses several strategies.
1 Words and expressions that appeal to the reader's common sense, e.g. *undoubtedly*.
2 Conjunctions to link ideas, e.g. *as a result*.
3 Time markers to build the argument toward a conclusion, e.g. *next*.

☐ After all ☐ At this point ☐ Finally
☐ Therefore ☐ As we all know ☐ By now
☐ However ☐ Nevertheless ☐ Moreover

D Connect the pairs of sentences logically, using the words or expressions in parentheses.
1 People love personal attention. Tips may be bigger if you give it. (as we all know, so)
2 I find it hard to say no. That's not such a good quality. (which, undoubtedly)
3 Friends understand us better than family. They tend to be more objective. (undoubtedly, and moreover)
4 My friends have persuaded me to be a little calmer. You'd never know I was once a nervous wreck. (since, at this point)

E Your turn! Choose a topic that you discussed in 10B and write a persuasive essay in 280 words.

Before
Using your notes from 10A, plan four to five paragraphs.

While
Write your essay, following the model in A. Include a clear thesis statement, and start a new paragraph for each sub-theme. Use strategies from *Write it right!* to build your argument.

After
Post your essay online and read your classmates' work. Whose is most convincing?

The psychology of persuasion

1 Persuasion involves just a little basic psychology, and this is true whether your target is a parent, a teacher, or even your boss. Research on the science of persuasion shows that we like people who are similar to us, pay us compliments, and cooperate with us. As a result, we are more likely to do what they request. How then can we apply this science in our everyday lives?

2 Let's look at an example, one we've all identified with at some point: How can we persuade our parents to give us more independence? Does this challenge have anything to do with being liked?

3 Undoubtedly, your first reaction will be "no." You may point out that your parents don't "like" you, they "love" you, and, not only that, their "love" is permanent. ¹_____, to agree to your request, they do need to "like" you at the moment you make it. ²_____, it is possible to "love" someone and not "like" the person at every given moment. So let's look at the research step by step.

4 Nothing pleases parents more than to think that they and their children are alike. ³_____, not only have they invested a lot of time and energy in your upbringing, but you are likely to be here when they're gone – their legacy on earth, so to speak. In the case of children, if they are just like their parents, this also implies shared values, and shared values imply trust. ⁴_____, if you think like your parents, you are less likely to make decisions they would be against. Let's take a case in point: You'd like to borrow the family car for a long weekend. What similarities between you and your parents come to mind? Most people will think being cautious is a character trait to emphasize. ⁵_____, you might start by saying, "You know how careful I am, Mom (or Dad). I'm just like you."

5 Next come praise and admiration. You may be opposed in principle to excessive praise and feel pouring it on is "false" or "manipulative." ⁶_____, is that necessarily so? What if the feeling is real? You might say, "I've always admired you, Dad (or Mom) for thinking things over so carefully. It shows you're open to considering all sides of an argument." Don't be surprised if your parent then announces that he or she admires this about you, too! Good feeling is being created all around, and you're well on your way to dissuading your Dad (or Mom) from saying "no."

6 ⁷_____, people who lend a helping hand seem reasonable and thoughtful. Your parents are more likely to be persuaded if you appear to have these traits. Here you might start by saying, "I know you get up really early on Mondays and don't want to spend Sunday evening worrying. So I promise I'll have the car back no later than 6:00 p.m." ⁸_____, all three principles of persuasion are in place, and the odds are clearly in your favor. ⁹_____, you're nearly guaranteed a "yes" answer!

113

Review 5
Units 9–10

1 Listening

A ▶R5.1 Listen to a professor discussing traditional and innovative learning. Check (✔) the statements that can be inferred. The professor probably feels …

1. ☐ traditional techniques can be made to be innovative.
2. ☐ good lectures require very knowledgeable speakers.
3. ☐ it's easier to take notes than to participate in class.
4. ☐ a lecture is more innovative if it incorporates video.
5. ☐ the virtues of lectures need to be promoted more.

B Make it personal In pairs, discuss which statements in A you agree with.

> There might be some truth to number 3.

> Yes, note-taking discourages us from participating actively.

2 Reading

A Read the article. Underline at least one sentence in each section where the writer could have been talking about children.

HOW TO SET GOOD LIMITS WITH FRIENDS

Setting limits with friends may be difficult, but just as you would with your children, the sooner you establish them, the better. A number of years back, we befriended a new couple in the neighborhood, who made it a habit to pay us a surprise visit every Saturday night. Had they not arrived with a delicious cake each time, we might have caught on sooner that they had an issue with boundaries. Here are a few pieces of advice based on this experience. They may not be innovative, but are known to work!

1 **Be direct.** If you're not clear, the other person may have trouble grasping what it is you're trying to communicate. Once you've planned what to say, go through with it, even if your message is that you find someone's behavior unacceptable.

2 **Avoid guilt and self-doubt.** Don't let a fictitious belief that "others come first" sabotage your legitimate need to act. Trust your instincts, which will outweigh any second thoughts you may have.

3 **Do not backpedal.** Despite the fact that you may have an overriding desire to please, don't allow yourself to be persuaded by your friends' point of view. In the end, they will appreciate your having held your ground. Consistency is every bit as important to friends as to children.

B Make it personal In pairs, discuss setting boundaries with friends. Is the advice in the article helpful? Use degrees of comparison where possible.

> I've followed point 1. The more honest you are, the closer you and your friends will be.

Review 5
9–10

3 Grammar

A Read the advice on how to lose weight. Complete 1–8 with the verbs in parentheses and grammar patterns from Lessons 9.2 and 9.4. Some have more than one answer.

Top three ways to lose weight

1. You might not believe this, but adding foods to your diet [1] *is known* to *have helped* (help, know) people lose weight! Healthy fruits and vegetables make great snacks and [2] _____ us _____ (appreciate, help) food even more.

2. Joining a gym may actually [3] _____ us _____ (avoid, cause) exercise, contrary to popular opinion. That's because "working out" sounds like work, so it [4] _____ us _____ (dislike, encourage) it. You may [5] _____ my _____ (appreciate, give) you the advice to just walk more. A fast-paced stroll [6] _____ to _____ (be, believe) boring, but that's rarely true!

3. Many people [7] _____ _____ (lose, think) weight just by drinking water. If that sounds odd, it's simply because it [8] _____ us _____ (feel, make) less hungry.

B Make it personal Choose two sentences and, in pairs, explain why you agree or disagree.

> I disagree with number 1. Adding foods may be known to have helped people lose weight, but it's so easy to add the wrong foods.

4 Writing

Write your opinion on one of these topics. Follow the model in **2A**, and include three pieces of advice.
- a Setting limits in relationships
- b Giving honest feedback
- c Asking a parent to respect your privacy

5 Self-test

Correct the two mistakes in each sentence. Check your answers in Units 9 and 10. What's your score, 1–20?

1. Adele strengthed her fan base and sold out every other performer.
2. In the past, these types of treatments are thought to help people even if it seems unlogical.
3. My angry reaction to what you said might have to see with you refuse to listen!
4. Unmatureness often makes children to think only about themselves.
5. I love my work so there's really no telling to why I'm looking forward to retire.
6. More friends you have, more happy you'll be.
7. Jim is quite as close to us than he used to be.
8. My uncle was the laughter of the party – a true breath of cool air!
9. You should wish to come, accommodating you isn't unsurmountable.
10. I'm far qualified than my résumé shows, and were you hire me, you wouldn't regret it.

6 Point of view

Choose a topic. Then support your opinion in 100–150 words, and record your answer. Ask a partner for feedback. How can you be more convincing?

- a Society should discourage women from raising children alone. OR Society should make single parenting easier.
- b Friends naturally drift apart after college. OR With a little effort, college friendships can be lifelong.
- c We're never more than six steps away from the perfect person. OR Meeting the perfect person depends largely on effort.

11

What was the last risk you took?

1 Vocabulary: Risk-taking expressions

A ▶ 11.1 Read the quiz and, using your intuition, complete the highlighted expressions with *safe*, *safety* or *caution*. Listen to two colleagues, Phil and Lisa, to check.

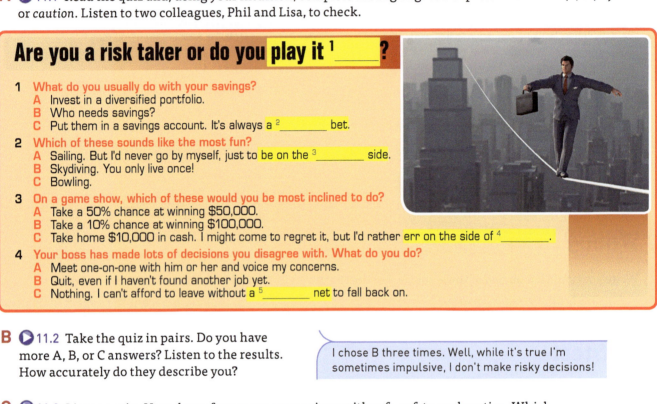

Are you a risk taker or do you play it ¹____?

1 What do you usually do with your savings?
  A Invest in a diversified portfolio.
  B Who needs savings?
  C Put them in a savings account. It's always a ² _____ bet.
2 Which of these sounds like the most fun?
  A Sailing. But I'd never go by myself, just to be on the ³ _____ side.
  B Skydiving. You only live once!
  C Bowling.
3 On a game show, which of these would you be most inclined to do?
  A Take a 50% chance at winning $50,000.
  B Take a 10% chance at winning $100,000.
  C Take home $10,000 in cash. I might come to regret it, but I'd rather err on the side of ⁴ _____.
4 Your boss has made lots of decisions you disagree with. What do you do?
  A Meet one-on-one with him or her and voice my concerns.
  B Quit, even if I haven't found another job yet.
  C Nothing. I can't afford to leave without a ⁵ _____ net to fall back on.

B ▶ 11.2 Take the quiz in pairs. Do you have more A, B, or C answers? Listen to the results. How accurately do they describe you?

> I chose B three times. Well, while it's true I'm sometimes impulsive, I don't make risky decisions!

C ▶ 11.2 Listen again. Note down four more expressions with *safe*, *safety*, and *caution*. Which expression(s) in A can you replace with them in context?

D Rephrase 1–5 using expressions from **A** and **C**. There may be more than one answer. Then make each sentence true for you.
  1 When I invite people over, I always end up cooking too much. Well, <u>it's better to do too much than too little</u>.
  2 If you want to have good Italian food, try Massimo's. <u>You can't go wrong</u> if you eat there.
  3 My friends say I should <u>stop being so careful</u>, quit my job, and have my own business.
  4 I always put away 10% of my paycheck every month. That way I'll have <u>some savings for a rainy day</u>.
  5 I love going to the gym. But I never work out more than an hour and always <u>take special care</u> to avoid injuring myself.

E Make it personal What makes people more / less prone to risk-taking?
  1 Individually, check the two most important factors. Note down a possible reason for each.
  2 In groups, share your thoughts. Any major disagreements?

☐ gender ☐ age ☐ upbringing ☐ job ☐ marital status ☐ zodiac sign ☐ _____

> For me, upbringing is most important. If you're taught to err on the side of caution, you'll be that way for life.

> I don't agree. You can learn not to play it safe.

116

Don't listen to a word I say. Hey! The screams all sound the same. Hey! Though the truth may vary. This ship will carry our bodies safe to shore

2 Listening

A ▶ 11.3 Listen to Phil tell Lisa about the promotion he's been offered. Order his concerns 1–4. There's one extra.

Phil fears he might …
- [ ] not be able to overcome the language barrier.
- [ ] lack leadership skills.
- [ ] not be good at the job.
- [ ] miss his family and friends.
- [ ] have trouble getting settled in a foreign country.

B ▶ 11.4 and 11.5 Read and listen to *Intonation and intentions*. Then listen to four pairs of excerpts. When you hear the beep, choose Lisa's response (a or b). Continue listening to check.

Intonation and intentions

Changes in intonation may convey completely different intentions and / or emotions:

Phil: Blame it on my upbringing.
Lisa: What do you mean? (= "Tell me more.")

Phil: I'm not sure I have what it takes … you know, to be a sales manager.
Lisa: What do you mean? (= "I disagree.")

1 "So …"   a [ ] Anyway …   b [ ] What's the problem?
2 "Oh, come on!" a [ ] Just say yes, please.   b [ ] Don't be silly!
3 "Of course."   a [ ] Without a doubt!   b [ ] Don't worry! You can trust me.
4 "What?"   a [ ] You've got to be kidding! b [ ] Please explain.

C Make it personal Get out of your comfort zone!

1 ▶ 11.6 **How to say it** Complete the chart. Listen to check.

| Expressing hesitation and encouragement ||
What they said	What they meant
Hesitation	
1 There's just too much at _____.	The risks are too high.
2 I'm not sure I have what it _____.	I might not have the necessary qualities.
3 I need to _____ on it.	I can't make a decision right now.
Encouragement	
4 What do you have to _____?	What could go wrong?
5 What's the worst that could _____?	What's the worst case scenario?
6 Why not just _____ with the flow?	Why not just take things as they come?

2 In pairs, role-play one of the situations below.
A: Choose a situation and note down three things that might go wrong.
B: Offer reassurance and try to get A out of his / her comfort zone.

What might you have to lose if you …?

spent all your savings on a great vacation   created your own YouTube channel
told an old friend you had feelings for him/her   started posting political views on Facebook
applied to sing in a reality show   adopted two puppies from a rescue organization

> I'd love to spend a month traveling across Europe, but things are kind of up in the air at work. There's too much at stake.

> Hmm … If you did go, what's the worst that could happen?

11.2 Do you enjoy riding a bike?

3 Language in use

A ▶ 11.7 Listen to a program on bike safety. It can be inferred that [**only the instructor has** / **both the instructor and participants have**] thought about safety before.

B ▶ 11.7 Use the pictures to guess the missing words in the safety tips. Then listen again to check.

BICYCLE SAFETY TIPS FROM OUR STAFF AND PARTICIPANTS

1. "You <u>might want to take</u> ☐ some basic precautions even when you're buying a new bike. Make sure the _____ of your _____ can support your _____."

2. "I <u>won't ride</u> ☐ my first day in a new city. I explore the area on _____ to be sure I won't have any _____ when I'm riding."

3. ☐ "The driver <u>could have looked</u> before opening his _____. It was a close call! If drivers are looking at all, it's only for _____. So be careful!"

4. "They all <u>should have mastered</u> ☐ the basics in a few days, but one _____ had poor _____. So don't be too hard on yourself."

5. "You <u>might try riding</u> ☐ only during the day at first. Then make sure to buy a _____. Your _____ is reduced at _____."

6. "It <u>shouldn't be hard to remember</u> ☐ one important rule, though. Always ride _____, and not _____ traffic."

C ▶ 11.8 Listen to an eyewitness account from two points of view. What safety rule did each person violate? Whose behavior is more dangerous?

D ▶ 11.9 Listen to excerpts 1–6 from the conversation. Choose the missing phrase or sentence below for each "beep". Continue listening to check.

☐ froze in her tracks
☐ My hair stood on end.
☐ screeched to a halt
☐ I could feel the color draining from my face.
☐ screamed at the top of my lungs
☐ swerved to avoid hitting me

E Make it personal Choose a situation. In pairs, role-play a real or imagined "eyewitness account." Use at least four expressions from D.

speeding bike or motorcycle   distracted pedestrian   child in the road   reckless bus or car driver

> You look shaken. What exactly happened?

> I sure am! You see, I was minding my own business and suddenly, I just froze in my tracks. This motorcycle was coming right at me!

♪ Oh, I would do anything for love. I would do anything for love, but I won't do that. No, I won't do that

11.2

4 Grammar: Special uses of modals

A Read the grammar box and complete the rule. Then write a–d in the boxes next to the underlined examples in 3B.

Special uses of modals: expectation, suggestion, refusal, and annoyance	
a expectation	It **shouldn't be** dangerous. I think it's safe.
	She **should have landed** by now. I'll check the flight online.
b suggestion	We **might as well forget** it then. We wouldn't be happy with a car that doesn't have the latest safety features.
	You **might want to take** some precautions. I've heard travel there is dangerous.
c refusal	He **won't listen** to me. I've told him to wear a bike helmet!
d annoyance	She **could have called** at least. I was really worried something had happened to her!

Modal verbs have more than one meaning. *Should* also expresses ¹o_____, *might* and *could* also express ²p_____, and *will* also describes a ³f_____ event.

» Grammar expansion p.158

B Using your completed grammar box in A, say the function expressed by each word in bold (1–8). Then make four sentences true for you.

OUR CITY, THE TRANSPORTATION BLOG

◆ You ¹**should** watch out for pedestrians at all times. These days, people are on their cell phones when they cross the street!

◆ It ²**shouldn't** be hard to learn to ride a motorcycle. It just involves good balance, like a bike.

◆ You ³**might** as well put your energy into bike, not car, safety. Pretty soon there's going to be nowhere to park around here.

◆ I'm afraid something ⁴**might** have happened to the plans for more traffic lights. The city is doing nothing!

◆ If I hadn't looked up, I ⁵**could** have been killed. The corner of 8th and Warren is the most dangerous intersection in the city.

◆ The cops ⁶**could** have been a little more understanding. It's hard to move your car after a snowstorm.

◆ Starting next year, there ⁷**won't** be any cars on Broom Street. They're turning it into a pedestrian walkway.

◆ I'm not letting my son drive until he's 21! He ⁸**won't** wear his seat belt, even though he knows it's illegal.

C What are the people saying? Complete 1–3 with appropriate modal verbs. Which items in B are they talking about?

1 A ticket! You _____ want to be a little more understanding. I _____ move my car until you plow this street!

2 Hey, watch out! You _____ have looked where you were going! It _____ be too hard to put that phone away for a second.

3 You _____ as well forget getting a license! And I _____ let you in the car with me in the future either!

D **Make it personal** In new pairs, role-play your situations from 3E again. This time, comment with special uses of modals in A.

> You won't believe what just happened. This motorcycle was coming right at me, and I had to jump out of the way.

> That's awful. He could have been a little more careful. They're always speeding through here.

119

11.3 Are you in favor of online dating?

5 Reading

A Read the article on online dating up to the heading "Big Mistake." In pairs, brainstorm possible reasons for the author's mistake. Then read the next paragraph to check. Are you surprised?

> I think she might have stolen something from his house.

B Make sure you understand the section titles below. Then read the rest. Put the titles back into the article (1–7).

> Ask the right questions   Be safe at home   Call for backup, Part 1   Call for backup, Part 2
> Gentlemen first   Know when to bail   Pick a safe spot for your first date

How to Stay Safe While Dating
by Ken Solin

Follow these tips to stay safe during your first few encounters with someone new

I was walking on California's Stinson Beach in August 2009 when I struck up a conversation with a woman who seemed utterly delightful. Captivated, I invited her to dinner at my house that evening.

Big mistake!
After dinner, she refused to leave. And, according to her, why should she? My acquaintance of 12 hours bizarrely insisted that we were living together. The situation felt menacing — would I find a rabbit stew boiling on the stove? — so I summoned my next-door neighbor, a woman, for help. The two of us spent 45 minutes coaxing my surprise head case to leave, but it took a threat to call the police to finally get her out the door.

Does it jar you to find a man writing about dating safety? Don't let it. Scary situations can pop up for anyone in the dating world — female or male, online or not. That's why everyone who is part of that world must take some basic steps to ensure his or her physical safety. At the very least, consider adopting the approaches below; all of them draw on my 12 years of recent online dating experience.

1 _____   When you've exchanged emails with a prospect and you feel it's time to furnish phone numbers, the man should offer his first. If he doesn't, the woman should ask him to do so. I can't think of any good reason why a legitimately eligible man would withhold his digits; if he does, that's ample cause to feel unsafe. Give the dude a pass.

2 _____   A busy daytime cafe is ideal. There isn't much privacy, but you'll be grateful for the presence of others if an unpleasant situation develops. If your date refuses to meet at a cafe or insists on a less public place, simply move on.

3 _____   I once had a coffee date with a woman who grew increasingly angry – and vocal – over her mistreatment by an ex-boyfriend. When she turned her attack on me, I got up and left – and was thankful for an audience to witness my exit.

4 _____   If a coffee date shows up with a bad attitude, a bad temper or a foul mouth, head for the door. Do likewise if he or she attempts to corral you into a relationship. If you feel truly threatened, explain the situation to the cafe manager and ask him or her to walk you to your car.

5 _____   I was enjoying a second date at a restaurant when my companion took a call during dinner. I was pretty sure I knew what was going on.
"I'm just fine," she told the caller, then stowed the phone with an apologetic smile.
"What would your friend have done if you hadn't picked up?" I asked her.
"She had instructions to call the police," she replied.
Good tip. Smart woman.

6 _____   Certain queries can reveal a lot of info in a short amount of time about a person you've just met. You might ask, for example, if your date has close friends: a "yes" indicates he or she is capable of connecting with others; a "no" suggests a lack of intimacy skills.

7 _____   As I learned the hard way with my would-be Glenn Close, it's unwise to welcome anyone into your abode unless you know them well. If you're unsure, consider asking another couple to join you.

♪ Heartbreaks and promises, I've had more than my share. I'm tired of giving my love, And getting nowhere

11.3

My current girlfriend (whom I met online, by the way) invited me into her home after only our second date. I accepted, thanking her for her trust, but later mentioned that she could have been putting herself at risk.

We all want to believe the best about people, but a date you don't really know deserves only a modicum of trust. So rather than rolling the dice when it comes to your personal safety, try following the steps above. Who knows? They might even be a shortcut to finding the right person out there.

Note: Dating services' official rules for dating online are located under their websites' terms of use. They suggest appropriate behavior, but screening is minimal – so I strongly urge you to use the tips above to create your own safety zone. Keep in mind that you can block any other member if you ever start to feel that safety is an issue.

C ▶ 11.10 Listen and re-read to check. Which tip do you think is most important?

D Make it personal What are the best safety rules? In groups, answer 1–3.
1 Should women and men follow the same safety advice? Why (not)?
2 Is any advice missing? Can you add at least one more piece?
3 What online dating safety stories have you heard or read about? Give advice. What new tips have you picked up?

> OK, let's see. Men need to be careful with their phone numbers, too.

6 Vocabulary: Whether to look up words

A Read *Deciding when to look up words*. Then re-read the sentences in the article where the yellow highlighted words appear. In pairs, explain whether you will look them up and why (not).

> **Deciding when to look up words**
>
> Stopping to look up lots of words decreases reading pleasure. Before looking up words, ask yourself these questions:
> 1 Have you seen the word before?
> **Yes** Go to question 2.   **No** It may be infrequent. Keep reading.
> 2 Is it necessary to understand the word?
> **Yes** Go to question 3.
> **No** The sentence makes sense. Keep reading.
> 3 Do you want to learn this word right now for active use?
> **Yes** Look it up. Find the meaning that matches the text.
> **No** Try to figure out the meaning from context and keep reading.

> *Coaxing* must come from the verb *coax*. I've never seen or heard it before, have you?

> No. But, following rule 3, let's not look it up. I wonder what it means, though.

> I think it might mean "to convince." It's pretty clear he's trying to get her to leave.

B ▶ 11.11 Listen to a conversation between two teachers and note down the words not chosen. Then find them among the blue highlighted words. Do you agree? If not, follow rule 3 in A.

C Make it personal Create your own safety tips! In groups, choose two topics and create five tips for each one. Use highlighted blue and yellow words where useful.

How to safely …

be a celebrity   go on a crash diet   become a political activist   be a police officer   hire employees

> First: If you want to be a celebrity, you might need to hire a bodyguard.

> Yes, strange situations can pop up!

121

11.4 What does the sea make you think of?

7 Listening

A In pairs, if you and saw this sign at the beach, would you go in the water? Why (not)?

B ▶ 11.12 Listen to a couple talking at the beach. Note down one convincing argument each person gives. Are you more like Bob or Andrea?

C ▶ 11.13 Which of these are more likely to kill you than a shark attack? Listen to check. Were you surprised?

1   2   3   4

D ▶ 11.14 Listen to the end of the conversation. Which reason 1–3 does Andrea give for saying that the numbers "can't be taken at face value"?

1 ☐ They don't take people's location into account.
2 ☐ Not all oceans have sharks.
3 ☐ The figures haven't been updated in a while.

8 Pronunciation: Stressing function words for emphasis

A ▶ 11.15 Read and listen to to the rules. Then read exchanges 1–4 and guess the stressed words in the responses.

> As we saw on page 67, auxiliaries may be stressed for emphasis. Other normally unstressed function words like conjunctions, articles, and pronouns, are sometimes stressed, too.
> BOB: You worry too much. Come on! Have some fun!
> ANDREA: I **am** having fun. But I want to have fun **and** be safe. And I want **you** to be safe, too.

1 ANDREA: Do you want to get eaten by a shark? ☐
　BOB: Do I want what?
2 ANDREA: There are an estimated 64 attacks each year, but few are fatal. ☐
　BOB: Few. Not none, so the odds might not be in our favor!
3 ANDREA: That doesn't make any sense! Sharks are color blind! ☐
　BOB: Color blind? They are?
4 ANDREA: It's written right here! The evidence is clear! ☐
　BOB: I think it's anything but clear.

B ▶ 11.16 Listen to check. In pairs, first repeat and then extend each exchange.

C **Make it personal** In pairs, choose a picture from **7C** and role-play a conversation where you don't agree on risk. Pay close attention to word stress.

A: You're extremely risk-averse.
B: You don't mind taking risks.

> Get away from that tree! You could be hit by lightning.

> I could be, but I won't be! What are the chances of that?

♪ Baby, this is what you came for. Lightning strikes every time she moves. And everybody's watching her, But she's looking at you

11.4

9 Grammar: Definite and indefinite articles

A Read the grammar box. Then write a–f next to mini-dialogues 1–4 in **8A**.

Definite and indefinite articles: general and specific uses		
general	a countable nouns	**Precautions** need to be taken.
	b non-count nouns	**Research** tells us that the risks are real.
specific	c first mention	Is this **a risk** you're willing to take?
	d adjective + number	**A record ten** attacks were recorded in 2016.
	e shared knowledge	**The study** was conducted in Japan.
	f adjective = group of people	**The rich** tend to live longer.

» Grammar expansion p.158

B Correct the mistakes in article use in some of the underlined phrases (1–8).

> **Common mistakes**
> *some / a piece of*   *advice is / suggestions are*
> Mark gave me ~~an~~ advice. His ~~advices are~~ always good.

Are you worrying about the right things?

> These days, it's hard to choose what to worry about. ¹Climate change? Resistant bacteria? ²The flu outbreaks? Whichever the answer, remember: Your brain is wired to conspire against you! Although ³human brain can respond well to risk, it's not good at deciding which modern threats are actually worth worrying about. This is because our survival instincts are activated by the choices that kept our ancestors safe, in ⁴a world where dangers took the form of ⁵predators, not terrorists. As a result, we tend overestimate the odds of rare events, such as ⁶the plane crashes, while downplaying the real risks, such as lack of exercise. According to a recent study, for example, ⁷an astounding 83 million Americans are living ⁸sedentary lifestyle.

C Read *Quantifiers and pronouns*. Then rephrase the underlined sentences in 1–5. Replace the bold words with those in parentheses.

Quantifiers and pronouns

Notice the pronoun differences between countable and non-count nouns.

Non-count	Countable
The article offers lots of **advice**.	The article offers lots of **suggestions**.
Most of **it** is useful, some of **it** is not.	Most of **them** are useful, some of **them** are not.
	One of **them** in particular is terrible.

1 <u>There are a lot of **studies** on cell-phone use, but how reliable are they?</u> (research) I keep worrying about the risks posed by the radiation.
2 Exactly! And <u>let's not forget the WiFi **devices** we're surrounded by and the radiation they emit.</u> (equipment)
3 The recent unemployment statistics are pretty scary, and I worry about losing my job. <u>Well-paid work isn't easy to come by these days.</u> (jobs)
4 <u>There seem to be competing **facts** about whether eggs are good for you.</u> (evidence) Why can't scientists decide?
5 <u>Digital songs are more affordable than they've ever been.</u> (music) How will artists make money?

D **Make it personal** In groups, which concerns do you share from **C**? What other concerns are important to you? Be careful with articles.

> Teen obesity is a major problem. I read that an astonishing 17 percent of teens are obese.

> Yes, schools need to pay more attention to teaching good nutrition.

123

11.5 Have you ever had an allergic reaction?

10 Listening

A ▶ 11.17 Listen to the beginning of a lecture on allergies. Complete the notes.

> Percent suffering in U.S. [1]_____ (Adults [2]_____ Children [3]_____)
> Three main causes of fatalities: 1) [4]_____ , 2) [5]_____ , 3) [6]_____
> Anaphylactic [7]_____ : Name comes from [8]_____

B ▶ 11.18 Listen to the second part and take notes. In pairs, share two important facts that you've learned. Were they similar?

> Anaphylactic shock can come on quickly. It's important to seek help immediately!

C ▶ 11.19 These symptoms are mentioned in the second part. In pairs, brainstorm other possible causes for them. Then listen to check. Were your ideas mentioned?

cramps   hives   sense of impending doom

swelling   itching   wheezing

> Wheezing, for example, might occur if you had asthma.

11 Keep talking

A In groups, choose a topic where you'd like to know more about safety. Choose from those below or think of your own.

> home safety   sailing / operating a boat   horseback riding
> side effects to everyday medications   hotel and vacation safety

B 🛜 Brainstorm three specific questions about your topic you don't know the answer to. Search online by entering each question in a search engine.

C Share your information with the class. Be sure to explain any new words. Which topic did you learn the most about?

> You shouldn't have any problems at a hotel if you make sure the entrance is in a well-lit area. Always err on the side of caution!

> Also check that your door has a dead-bolt lock. That means one that has a heavy sliding bar that moves when you turn it.

♪ I've been through the desert on a horse with no name. It felt good to be out of the rain

11.5

12 Writing: A statistical report

A Read the report, underlining the numbers. Which is the most surprising fact?

B Read *Write it right!* Then complete 1–5 with a singular or plural form of the verb in parentheses. Read the report again to check.

> **Write it right!**
>
> When you use numbers, subject–verb agreement can be tricky. Here are three rules to help you:
> 1. When you use fractions, percentages, or words like *half*, *some*, *most*, and *all*, the **object** of the preposition determines the verb:
>   Two thirds / 70% of the **voters are** undecided.
>   Half / Most of the **information** I got **is** useless.
> 2. After *one*, the verb is always singular:
>   **One** out of every three homes **has** Netflix.
> 3. *The number* takes a singular verb. *A number*, which means *many*, takes a plural verb:
>   **The number** of people with allergies **is** high.
>   And **a number** of them **have** severe reactions.

1. Seven percent of children _____ allergies. (have)
2. A number of studies _____ that the number of children _____ rising. (be)
3. One in every 13 children under 18 _____ affected by allergies. (indicate, be)
4. In the U.S., many of the most common allergic reactions _____ from fish allergies. (come)
5. Three out of every 15 people with allergies _____ peanut and tree nut allergies. (report)

C Imagine you've been asked to write a statistical report on one of the topics in 11A to a specific audience responsible for safety, such as insurance companies, vacation resorts, or doctors. Your report will need to highlight possible dangers and give recommendations.

Before
🌐 Choose your audience and plan two charts to support your message. Search on questions designed to produce statistics, such as "How many people …?"

While
Write three to four paragraphs to summarize your charts, following the model in A. Address your audience in paragraph 1 and give recommendations in the conclusion. Use expressions with numbers from *Write it right!*, paying careful attention to subject-verb agreement.

After
Post your report online and read your classmates' work. Whose statistics best supported the report?

FOOD ALLERGIES:
please read carefully

Five out of every 100 Americans have food allergies – that's an astonishing 15 million people, or close to 4%. What's more, the rate is even higher in children. One in every 13 children under the age of 18 is affected. In other words, on average, over 7% of children have food allergies. In addition, a number of studies indicate that the number of children is steadily rising. Teachers: please review this information carefully.

Only eight foods account for 90 percent of these allergic reactions: milk, eggs, peanuts, tree nuts (walnuts, almonds, hazelnuts, cashews, etc.), soy, wheat, fish, and shellfish. Yet these foods can be very dangerous. Food allergies may cause anaphylactic shock, a sudden reaction that, if not treated quickly, may be fatal.

By age, allergies in children and teenagers break down as follows:

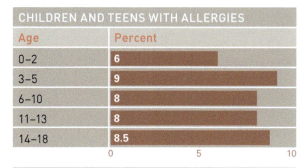

Among those diagnosed, the scope of the problem can be seen in this chart:

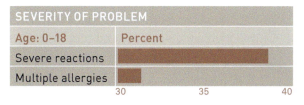

Some allergies can be outgrown, but fish and shellfish allergies are usually lifelong. In the U.S., many of the most common allergic reactions come from fish allergies – more than 6.5 million adults have them. Peanut and tree nut allergies tend to be lifelong also. More than three million adults report such allergies. Alarmingly, food allergies overall are so common that, in the U.S., someone ends up in the emergency room every three minutes, for a total of 200,000 visits a year.

Epinephrine auto-injectors can save lives! Should you be faced with an emergency, do not attempt to treat a student yourself. Take him or her immediately to the nurse's office and call 911. Every minute counts.

12 ⟫ What brands are the wave of the future?

1 Listening

A ▶ 12.1 Look at the cartoon. What do you think the professor's lecture will be about? Listen to check.

> Maybe he / she will talk about how bad the economy is right now.

B ▶ 12.1 Listen again. Check (✔) the points the professor makes.
1. ☐ Innovation involves risk-taking.
2. ☐ It's hard to change well-established practices.
3. ☐ Companies spend many years planning changes.

"What if we don't change at all … and something magical just happens?"

C ▶ 12.2 Listen to part two. Correct the mistake in each line of the student's notes.

Microsoft
1. 80s & 90s: high profits due to ~~PC~~ *software* sales
2. Mid 2000s – present: huge drop in computer sales, esp. laptops
3. *Surface* tablet: impressive sales at first
4. Future of PCs: 3D gaming won't increase sales

D ▶ 12.3 Listen to part three and complete the notes. Were your surprised?

National Geographic
1. Early days: American _____
2. Challenge in the 90s: number of _____ went down
3. John Fahey's role: change _____ of company
4. Digital presence: top non-celebrity account on _____

E 🌐 **Make it personal** Brands that have come and gone! In groups, do 1–3.
1. Individually, search on "brands that disappeared" to find an interesting story.
2. Read the case study and quickly note down the key points.
3. Share your stories. What should each company have done differently?

> Here's one … the amazing story of Blockbuster, the video rental company. They turned down a partnership with Netflix. Can you believe it?

126

♪ The world I love. The trains I hop, To be part of, The wave can't stop. Come and tell me when it's time to

12.1

2 Vocabulary: Verbs describing trends

A ▶12.4 Match the two halves. Listen to check. Then write the highlighted verbs under each graph.

1 Since the mid 2000s, sales of cell phones and tablets have increased worldwide,
2 The *Surface* line had a bumpy start,
3 If 3D gaming remains popular,
4 It seems the magazine had lost of some its edge,
5 National Geographic is the top non-celebrity account on Instagram,

a ☐ the decline in PC sales might **level off**.
b ☐ and the number of followers continues to **soar** month after month!
c ☐ but its sales eventually **skyrocketed**.
d ☐ while PC shipments have **plummeted**.
e ☐ and the number of subscribers began to **plunge**.

1

2

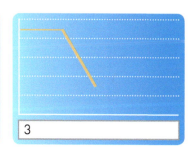
3

B Form sentences using cues 1–6. Notice the *Common mistake*.

Good news from around the globe:

1 Canada: number / traffic deaths / plunge / since 2006
2 Spain: unemployment / fall / from 2013 to 2016
3 India: generation of solar electricity / soar / over the past few years
4 UK life expectancy / rise / since 1990
5 U.S. obesity rates / men / level off / in 2016
6 Globally: poverty / plummet / in the last two decades

Common mistake

have
Sales ∧ plunged in / over the last three years.

C Make it personal Discuss trends in your region.

1 ▶12.5 **How to say it** Complete the chart. Listen to check.

Expressing cause and reason	
What they said	What they meant
1 (Many bankruptcies) _____ from (fear).	Negative outcome A is caused by B.
2 (Innovation) is _____ related to (risk and uncertainty).	A has a lot to do with B.
3 (Mobile computing) has _____ rise to (new challenges).	A has caused B.
4 (The TV channel) paved the _____ for (other innovations).	A made B possible.

2 In groups, change 1–6 in **B** to give true information for your region. Use expressions from **C** to explain the possible reasons. Can you think of any other trends?

> The number of traffic deaths around here has soared.
> It probably stems from raising the speed limit.

127

12.2 What songs have changed the world?

3 Language in use

A ▶12.6 Listen to a podcast about music and society. Note down one reason why each song below was influential.

Believe, Cher, 1998

Do They Know It's Christmas, Band Aid, 1984

B ▶12.6 Listen again. Check (✔) the points the music critic makes.
1. ☐ Most singers use Auto-Tune these days, which is objectionable.
2. ☐ Auto-Tune has made singers less unique.
3. ☐ Fundraising songs should be as catchy as possible.
4. ☐ Music may have lost some of its impetus for social change.

C ▶12.7 Complete 1–5 with a form of the highlighted phrasal verbs. Listen to check.

> **bring about**: make something happen
> **catch on**: become popular
> **fall back on**: use as a last resort
> **get across**: make an idea clear or convincing
> **grow on**: become more appealing over time
> **warm up to**: begin to like something or someone

1. Cher didn't refuse to be "auto-tuned," and the song instantly _____.
2. Today, most people – regardless of talent – can take a shot at singing if they can _____ Auto-Tune. It makes you wonder if singers are just one step away from being completely replaced by robots.
3. *Do they know …?* wasn't a tune I instantly _____, and I remember being underwhelmed when I first heard it.
4. But the song eventually _____ me, maybe because of the message it was trying to _____.
5. What's remarkable about *Do they know …?* is that it showed artists their influence could be used to _____ real change.

D Read *Transitive and intransitive phrasal verbs*. Then write 1–3 next to the phrasal verbs in **C**.

> **Transitive and intransitive phrasal verbs**
>
> Phrasal verbs can be transitive or intransitive:
> 1. Intransitive phrasal verbs don't take an object: Why did Abba **break up**?
> 2. Transitive ones need an object. Many are separable: They **called** the concert **off** / **called off** the concert.
> 3. Others are inseparable, including most three-word phrasal verbs: Can we **go over** the contract once more? (NOT ~~go the contract over~~); I'm **looking forward to** their next release.

♪ I want to thank you for giving me the best day of my life. Oh just to be with you is having the best day of my life

12.2

E Make it personal In groups, agree on your two favorite quotes. Explain what they mean and why you like them.

1 "Music and the music business are two different things." (Erykah Badu)
2 "There are two means of refuge from the miseries of life: music and cats." (Albert Schweitzer)
3 "The trade of critic, in literature, music, and ... drama, is the most degraded of all trades." (Mark Twain)
4 "Independent artists and labels have always been the trend setters in music and the music business." (Shawn Fanning)

> In the first one, I think she means that the music business is motivated by profit.

4 Grammar: Passive forms with gerunds and infinitives

A Read the grammar box. Underline the four passive sentences in 3C and write 1–6 next to each one.

Passive forms with gerunds and infinitives: after parts of speech and as subjects	
Use gerunds ...	Use infinitives and base forms ...
1 after certain verbs: Cher **enjoyed being played** on the radio again.	4 after certain verbs: Band Aid **hoped to be remembered** for the song.
2 after prepositions: She didn't object **to being "auto-tuned."**	5 after adjectives, nouns, and indefinite pronouns: The song is **unlikely to be forgotten**.
3 as subjects: **Being considered** cool again was her goal.	6 after modals: Its lyrics **should** not **be taken** at face value.
In negative sentences, the preferred form for *not* is before the infinitive: The singer was **disappointed not to be** invited to join the group.	

B Rewrite 1–6 in the passive, using *be*, *to be*, or *being*. Which books, if any, would you like to read?

Grammar expansion p.160

BOOKS THAT CHANGED THE WAY I ...

● **SET PRIORITIES:** *THE ONE THING*, BY GARY KELLER.
Do yourself a favor and read *The One Thing*. In it, the author shows us ¹why people should set priorities in the first place, and ²how we can accomplish this important task.

● **COPE WITH STRESS:** *HOW TO STOP WORRYING AND START LIVING*, BY DALE CARNEGIE.
I read this book at a very stressful moment in my life. ³I was so upset they didn't consider me for my dream job. Thanks to this book, I was able to pull myself together.

● **READ POETRY:** *TRANSFORMATIONS*, BY ANNE SEXTON.
Up until recently, if someone asked me whether I enjoyed reading poetry, I'd usually reply: ⁴"I'd prefer someone forced me to read the small print on a cereal box". But *Transformations*, which turns well-known fairy tales into poems, taught me how to appreciate it!

● **FEEL ABOUT READING:** *20,000 LEAGUES UNDER THE SEA*, BY JULES VERNE.
Over the years I've learned that ⁵having people tell you what to read is a surefire way to make you hate books! *20,000 Leagues ...* was the very first book I chose to read, and this made all the difference! ⁶I still recall that the author surprised me because I hadn't known that science fiction could be so engaging.

C Make it personal In pairs, has a book / movie / play / article ever had an impact on the way you ...?

approach friendships / romance   cope with stress   deal with money   have fun   see the world

> I don't remember ever being that influenced by a single book or movie. How about you?

> Actually, *Eat, Pray, Love* made me rethink my work schedule!

12.3 What futuristic programs have you seen?

5 Reading

A Imaginative drawings of the future were once common. Look at two postcards of "future" transportation. In pairs, answer 1–2.

1 Where could the people be going?
2 What else might artists have imagined 100 years ago?

> Well, the first one looks like a flying train. Aren't they on top of a building?

B ▶ 12.8 Read and listen to the article. Underline details describing how the future will be. Which (if any) do you see in A? Are you surprised by anything in the article?

Here's how people 100 years ago thought we'd be living today

In 100 years, there will be flying taxis and people will travel to the moon routinely. Knowledge will be instilled into students through wires attached to their heads. These may sound like the predictions of modern-day futurists, but they're how people a century ago saw the future – otherwise known to you and me as the present.

These vintage European postcards illustrate a view of the 21st century that is remarkably prescient in some ways and hilariously wrong in others, says Ed Fries, who selected them from his private collection.

In the 10 years since he left Microsoft, where he was co-founder of the Xbox project, Fries has worked on what he calls "a random collection of futuristic projects." He's advised or served on the board of companies working on 3-D printing, depth-sensing cameras (like those used in Kinect), and headsets for reading brain waves. Earlier this month, he presented some of his favorite postcards at a neurogaming conference in San Francisco, using them to illustrate pitfalls in predicting the future that remain relevant today.

One thing you see in the cards is a tendency to assume some things won't change, even though they undoubtedly will. In one image, a couple flags down an aerotaxi. That's futuristic enough, but the man is wearing spats and carrying a cane, while she has a parasol and an enormous hat with a feather. Did they really think transportation would undergo a revolution while fashion stayed frozen in time? "In every one of these you see a mix of a futuristic concept with stuff that looks to us to be very old fashioned," Fries said.

At the same time, there's virtually no hint in the postcards of the truly transformative technologies of the last century – namely personal computers and the Internet. Sure, there are video phones, but the image is projected on a screen or a wall. Moving pictures were just coming into existence, Fries says, so that wasn't a huge leap. But the idea of a screen illuminated from within seems to have been beyond their imagination.

All in all, people at the turn of the 20th century did a pretty good job of extrapolating the technology of their time, Fries says. But their imagination was limited by the world they lived in. The same is true today – at least for those of us who aren't the visionaries of tomorrow.

Fries thinks what sets those farsighted people apart has something to do with ignoring conventional wisdom. "The future is changed by people who have a crazy idea and follow it wherever it may lead," he said. "That's why I like hanging out with wacky people like at that neurogaming conference. One of them is probably going to change the world."

♪ Good friends we've lost along the way. In this great future, you can't forget your past. So dry your tears I say ...

12.3

C **Make it personal** In groups, search on "vintage postcards of the future." Share your favorite one.

> Here's one that's cool: a ship that turns into a train with wheels once it hits land. I wonder why those were never invented.

6 Vocabulary: Using a dictionary

A Read *Looking up words* and study the definition of *leap*. Answer 1–2.
1 Which questions from the box can be answered from the definition below?
2 Look up *leap* in a monolingual dictionary and find the noun. Is it countable or uncountable? How do you say, "We took a chance"?

Looking up words

When looking up words, follow these helpful guidelines:
1 Study the examples, and consider these questions: and consider these questions:
   (a) Which prepositions are possible? (b) Does the word seem formal or informal?
   (c) Does it have a figurative meaning, too?
2 Pay attention to collocations. What other words does the new word go with?
3 Decide the part of speech. Is the word a noun? If yes, is it countable or uncountable?

---

leap /liːp/ **verb** Other forms: **leaped** /liːpt/ **or leapt** /lɛpt/; also **leaping**
1 to jump from a surface **2** to jump over something **3** to move quickly
Examples:
1 He leaped from the bridge.
2 He leaped over the wall.
3 The cat leaped into the air. / We leaped at the chance. (fig)

B Choose five highlighted words from **5B** to look up. In pairs, explain what you learned.

> I chose *farsighted* and learned it has both a medical and figurative meaning ...

C **Make it personal** In groups, plan and draw your own futuristic postcard! Consider 1–3. Use highlighted words from **5B**.
1 Study the postcards in **5A** again. How might these areas be different?
2 Can you imagine fashion 100 years from now? Or would you prefer to draw current fashions like the postcard artists did?
3 Will there be anything truly transformative by 2050?

Jobs
Energy
Fashion
Transportation

> I know it might sound a little wacky, but I think we should draw a ...

131

12.4 How unpredictable has your life been?

7 Language in use

A ▶12.9 What do you know about these people? Read the website and guess the missing words. Listen to check.

THESE 19TH CENTURY AUTHORS FOUND THE UNEXPECTED!

1 Charles Dickens never would have imagined his ¹_____. Since his father couldn't pay his debts, he **got arrested** in 1824 and **got thrown in** debtor's prison. His whole family, including Charles, **had** their home **taken away** and had to join the father in ²_____. Then, as a young man, the future ³_____ **was exposed** to terrible ⁴_____ conditions in a factory. As a result, he soon had a wealth of ⁵_____ for his 15 novels, among them *Great Expectations* and *A Tale of Two Cities*. It turned out the hardships of his youth were worth it.

2 George Sand did not find what she was ⁶_____ when she traveled to the island of Mallorca, in the winter of 1838, with Polish ⁷_____ Frédéric Chopin. Sick with tuberculosis, Chopin **was being treated** in France, but **was getting pressured** by his doctor to find a milder ⁸_____. He thought a stay in Mallorca would be well worth the effort. They **had** their wishes **fulfilled** when they found a beautiful house in the town of Valldemossa. But, ⁹_____ for Chopin, he couldn't **get** his ¹⁰_____ **cured** because the humidity actually worsened it, and the couple had to return to France. Sand, though, now had material for a book: *A Winter in Mallorca*.

B Answer 1–6. Which story did you find more surprising?

Who ...
1 wasn't able to pay his or her debts?
2 lost their home and went to prison?
3 experienced bad working conditions?
4 encouraged Chopin to find a new climate?
5 was happy to find a beautiful house?
6 was still sick upon returning to France?

> I found the Dickens story shocking. I had no idea that he'd spent time in prison.

C ▶12.10 Read *Expressions with worth*. Then listen to two conversations about *Great Expectations*. Answer 1–2, using the expressions in the box.

Expressions with *worth*

Worth expressions usually imply there's value in the effort involved. The expressions are often interchangeable. However, if you're not expressing effort, *worth* can sound unnatural. Compare:

Is it **worth it** to read this long book? It's 600 pages!

Let's go to Henry's for dinner. The food is really ~~worthwhile~~ **good**.

| be worth it   be worth the effort / trouble   be worth + verb + -ing |
| be worth someone's time   be worthwhile |

Common mistake

It's
~~It~~ worth being frugal.

1 In conversation 1, why might the book a good choice for Mike?
2 In conversation 2, why might it not be a good choice?

D Make it personal In groups, have you ever done something you never thought would be worthwhile that led to an unpredictable result? Use expressions from C. Whose story is most surprising?

> I never thought it would be worth the effort to join a theater group. But I ended up getting the lead in a play!

♪ And I'm in so deep. You know I'm such a fool for you. You've got me wrapped around your finger. Do you have to let it linger?

12.4

8 Grammar: The passive and causative with *get*

A Read the grammar box. Then rephrase the verbs with *get* in **7A** with a form of *have* or *be*, and the ones with *have* or *be* with a form of *get*.

The passive with *get* and *be*; the causative with *get* and *have*

Passive: *get* = *be*	Tom	**was getting** **is being**	**hassled** **pressured**	a lot by his boss. to resign.
	I	**got** **was**	**fired** **left**	on Tuesday. without a job.
Causative passive: *get* = *have*	She	**got** **had**	her short story **accepted** her photo **taken**	by the magazine. as a result.
	We	**'ll be getting** **might have**	more work **assigned** our vacations **taken**	soon! away.

» Grammar expansion p.160

B Read *Spoken grammar: Using the get passive*. Then rephrase the underlined parts of 1–5 with a *get* passive or causative. In pairs, A: Read a sentence with emotion; B: Respond with feeling! Change roles.

Spoken grammar: Using the *get* passive

The *get* passive and causative, in spoken English, often convey nuances of meaning and register. For example:

a informality: Guess what! I **got accepted** into Harvard!
b emphasis: You **could get hurt** if you keep that up!
c negative intent: I **got** my wallet **stolen** as I was walking home.
d unintended consequence: Do you want to **get** me **arrested**?

1 Hey, you're going 90 miles an hour! Slow down. <u>Do you want us to die</u>?
2 Ouch! <u>Some creep just stepped on my foot</u>! I think he did it on purpose!
3 What! You're reading your boss's email? <u>She could fire you</u> and with good reason!
4 Fantastic news! <u>They awarded me</u> first prize for my painting!
5 Firecrackers are illegal! Do you want <u>the neighbors to take me to court</u>?

> Hey, you're going 90 miles an hour! Slow down. Do you want us to get killed?

> I'm sorry! I'm just worried we might miss our flight.

C ▶ 12.11 Guess what happened in pictures 1–4. Then listen to four conversations. After the "beep," rephrase the sentence with *get*. Continue listening to check.

D Make it personal In pairs, using only the pictures, role-play new situations. Use the passive or causative with *get*.

> Big news! I got my picture taken for the newspaper!

> You did? That's awesome.

12.5 What will make a better society?

9 Listening

A ▶ 12.12 Listen to the start of a lecture on building a utopian society. In pairs, answer Professor Orwell's question.

B ▶ 12.13 Listen to part two. Complete Jennifer's reasons. In pairs, are any convincing?

There will be no ...
1 housing shortage because buildings will be _____.
2 food shortage because people will have _____.
3 pollution because everyone will have a _____ for transportation.

> I think ... sounds ridiculous!

C ▶ 12.14 Listen to part three and take notes. Give one argument to show how ...
1 the housing crisis may diminish.
2 hunger will remain a problem.

D ▶ 12.15 Read *Whatsoever*. Then add *whatsoever* to 1–6, only if possible. Listen to check.

> **Whatsoever**
>
> Like *at all*, *whatsoever* can be used to emphasize negative ideas. Notice its position in these sentences:
>
> I have **no** idea **whatsoever** what a utopian society is.
>
> There's **nothing whatsoever** we can do to change the current situation.
>
> It can also be used in questions with *any*:
>
> Is there **any** doubt **whatsoever** that climate change is getting worse?

1 But rest assured, there's no connection to the famous novel, *1984*.
2 To me, a true utopia makes life just enjoyable and worth living.
3 I have no doubt that those things will come, too.
4 For one thing, the housing shortage will disappear.
5 There won't be any emissions where we live.
6 Is there any evidence that any of these changes might actually come about?

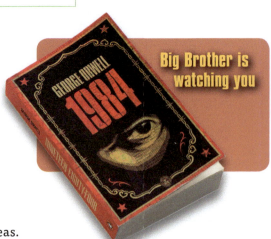

10 Keep talking

A In your view, is the world getting better or worse? Choose three areas.

> access to quality education   animal rights   international relations
> environmental issues   hunger   public health / homelessness

B 🛜 Note down reasons. Can you find any evidence to support your opinion?

C In groups, share your ideas. Any disagreements?

> I think the world is getting worse. For example, homelessness is on the rise.

> Hmm ... What's your evidence?

♪ If you wanna make the world a better place, Take a look at yourself, and then make a change

12.5

11 Writing: An opinion essay

A Read Oscar's essay in response to Professor Orwell's question. In your opinion, is he ...
1. ☐ convincing?
2. ☐ somewhat convincing?
3. ☐ not convincing?

B Complete the essay with words from **10A**.

C Read *Write it right!* Then rephrase 1–5 using verb or noun phrases. Scan the essay to check.

> **Write it right!**
>
> Good writers know how to use words and structures flexibly to avoid repetition. Verb phrases can be written as noun phrases without a change in meaning:
>
> | Verb phrase (verb + adverb) | Noun phrase (adjective + noun) |
> |---|---|
> | CO_2 levels have **risen steadily**. | There has been **a steady rise** in CO_2 levels. |
> | Average earnings **dropped slightly**. | There was **a slight drop** in average earnings. |

1. Life expectancy has increased steadily.
   There's been a steady increase in life expectancy.
2. International relations have improved slowly but steadily.
3. There's been a significant decrease in the number of international conflicts.
4. The planet's temperature has risen steeply.
5. Homelessness has fallen sharply in some places.

D **Your turn!** Write an opinion essay in response to Professor Orwell's question in about 280 words.

Before
Decide how optimistic you feel about the future of the world. Then choose two to three issues from **10A** and, using your notes, plan the content of each paragraph.

While
Write a four to five paragraph essay, following the model in **A**. Refer to *Write it right!* to vary your use of noun and verb phrases.

After
Post your essay online and read your classmates' work. What were the most pressing issues?

Is the world getting better or worse?

Let's face it. This year hasn't been the most positive of years. Last year was tough, too. But is the world really getting worse? When our social media feeds are filled with bad news after bad news, reasons for optimism can seem few and far between. However, if we look at the world as a whole, as opposed to individual countries, in my view things are actually getting better.

Take [1]_____ for example. Although access to health care is still an issue in many countries, recent advances in stem-cell research, gene therapy, and nanotechnology mean we're inching closer to a cure for diseases such Alzheimer's, Parkinson's, and multiple sclerosis, as well as some forms of cancer. There's also been a sharp fall in homelessness in some places. All of this might help to explain why there has been a steady increase in life expectancy.

Second, there has been a slow but steady improvement in [2]_____. Since World War II, the world has seen no "Great Wars," and the number of international conflicts has decreased significantly. Some historians refer to the period we are living in as the "Long Peace." While I don't quite agree since the world is still a dangerous place, in the long run, I feel globalization will make it safer.

We're still faced with serious [3]_____. In the past two decades, there's been a steep rise in the planet's temperature, which has caused glaciers to melt and seas to rise at unprecedented rates. The continued destruction of the Earth's biosphere and the extinction of an ever-increasing number of species are just some of the daunting challenges we're up against. Will we be able to meet them? Only time will tell, but at least awareness has increased.

Yet, despite all the problems in the world today, it doesn't seem as if we're on the edge of the apocalypse – at least not yet. In fact, looking back through the lens of history, it would seem to me that the opposite might be closer to the truth.

Review 6
Units 11–12

1 Listening

A ▶ R6.1 Listen to a conversation between two friends, Phil and Melinda. Her primary tone is ...
  a angry and sarcastic.   b angry, but resigned.   b sarcastic, but hopeful.

B ▶ R6.1 Listen again and fill in the modal verbs. Then match them with their functions (a–e).
  1 He _____ have just asked.
  2 You _____ want to file a report.
  3 This _____ be a bad corner.
  4 They _____ come here.
  5 It _____ be that hard to locate it.
  6 He _____ have at least dropped the bag.

  a ☐ possibility
  b ☐ suggestion
  c ☐ expectation
  d ☐ annoyance
  e ☐ refusal

C In pairs, role-play Phil and Melinda's conversation from memory.

> Stop, thief! Can you believe it? I just got my purse snatched!

2 Speaking

A Look at the cartoon on p.126.

  1 In two minutes, note down as many possible trends that you can imagine over the next ten years, using these words and expressions:

> a steady increase   a steep rise   be closely related to   bring about   drop slightly   give rise to   level off   plummet   plunge   rise significantly   skyrocket   soar   stem from

  2 In groups, share ideas. Similar opinions?

> Homelessness is going to skyrocket. There's not enough housing.

> Actually, I think it's likely to level off. Doesn't at least some of it stem from the recession?

B **Make it personal** Choose three question titles from Units 11 and 12 to ask a partner. Ask at least three follow-up questions for each. What did you learn about each other?

> What does the sea make you think of?

> Jellyfish! I'm always getting stung by them when I go swimming.

3 Writing

Write a persuasive paragraph summarizing three trends you predict from 2A.

  1 Note down evidence. 🛜 Search online for one key fact about each trend, as necessary.
  2 Express your arguments using verbs from the box. Change some to nouns to vary the wording.

> decrease   drop   fall   improve   increase   level off   rise

"There will be a dramatic increase in salaries."

4 Grammar

A Add or delete articles (1–9) where needed. Check (✔) those that are correct.

> Is there any doubt whatsoever that we have ¹homeless problem in the U.S.? ²A random study even showed that people walk by ³the homeless without even looking. Participants who saw ⁴the relatives on the street didn't even recognize them when they were disguised as ⁵the homeless people! Nevertheless, every two years, ⁶number of efforts is made in the U.S. to count the number of homeless in major cities. ⁷Last survey shows ⁸a staggering 578,424 people were without ⁹the shelter.

B In pairs, explain why the items are correct or incorrect.

> Number 1 is incorrect. It has to be a homeless problem. It's the first time it's been mentioned.

5 Self-test

Correct the two mistakes in each sentence. Check your answers in Units 11 and 12. What's your score, 1–20?

1. When trying out a new recipe, I always play it safety since there's no safe net to fall back on.
2. We can't just do with the flow because there's much at stake.
3. Susan gave me some well-intended advice, but actually, most of them aren't too useful.
4. Apparently, one out of every three people have the itching when stung by a bee.
5. I really warmed up Auto-Tuning and didn't even realize they'd fallen it back on.
6. I enjoy to be recorded when I sing and don't hope to make any errors.
7. My brother was being hassle by his boss, and then he got fire on Thursday.
8. The new restaurant is expensive but worth, and the food is really worth the trouble.
9. There's nothing whatever we can do about the steady rising in pollution here.
10. We're having pressured more by new boss more than ever.

6 Point of view

Choose a topic. Then support your opinion in 100–150 words, and record your answer. Ask a partner for feedback. How can you be more convincing?

a You think upbringing determines whether you're open to risk-taking. OR
   You think age is the most important factor in risk-taking.

b You think online dating is generally safe and you should go with the flow. OR
   You think online dating calls for detailed safety precautions.

c You think books are more influential than music in changing the world. OR
   You think the power of music in promoting social change shouldn't be underestimated.

d You think limited access to quality education is a major social problem. OR
   You think access to quality education has been steadily improving.

Grammar expansion

1 Summary of future tenses (do after 7.2)

The future perfect emphasizes the completion of an action and is often used with *by the time*. The future perfect continuous always implies the action is ongoing.

By the time I retire, I **will have had** at least three careers.

Unlike my parents, when I'm 90, I **will have been using** Facebook my whole life.

Going to and *will* are both used to make predictions. Use *going to* when you're more certain about your prediction or have present evidence. Always use a perfect tense with *for* and *since*.

A few years from now, our government **is going to run out** of money.

By 2050, people **will** still **be working** when they're 80.

By the time I'm 80, I **will have lived** here *for* 50 years because I have no intention of ever moving.

In the future, people **will have been telecommuting** *since* their very first job.

Common mistake

By the end of the century, 90-year-olds ~~will use / will be using~~ social media for many years.
will have used / will have been using

2 More formal uses (do after 7.2)

The future perfect or future perfect continuous is sometimes used to speculate about past events and is usually more formal than the present perfect or present perfect continuous.

| Neutral | No doubt you**'ve seen** that movie already and **have been telling** everyone else to do the same. |
| More formal | No doubt you **will have been** impressed by the performance and **will have been listening** to the orchestra's recordings. |

When predicting the future, you may omit the word *going* for a more formal sentence. A contracted sentence is not as formal.

| Neutral | If we**'re going to be** happy in our old age, we need to focus on our relationships. (active)
 If we think we**'re going to be rewarded** for living to 100, think again! (passive) |
| More formal | If I**'m** ever **to graduate**, I'd better start studying. (active)
 If we **are to live** longer, we need to change our eating habits. (active)
 Benefits **are to be paid** beginning at 65. (passive) |

3 Cleft vs. pseudo-cleft sentences (do after 7.4)

English has many ways to move information to the front of a sentence for emphasis. Sentences beginning with words like *what*, *when*, and *where* are called "pseudo-cleft" sentences.

Cleft sentences	It's younger people	who / that have a few things to learn. (subject)
	It's the unimaginable	(that) no one can predict. (object)
Pseudo-cleft sentences	When I'm really tired	is on the weekends.
	What I thought I once wanted	has all changed now.

150

1A Circle the correct forms.

Since I come from a family with lots of longevity, I ¹[**'ll live** / **'m going to live**] to be 100. When I ²[**will start** / **start**] my second century, I hope I ³[**will still be able** / **will have still been able**] to ride a bike. By that point, I ⁴[**will have earned** / **will have been earning**] the distinction of having been an avid cyclist for over 90 years, and I ⁵[**will have been participating** / **will have participated**] in at least 2,000 bike races! I ⁶[**won't be racing** / **won't have been racing**] any longer in my second century, and I ⁷[**won't have been giving** / **won't have been given**] any medals, but I ⁸[**will have been passing** / **will have passed**] the longevity test. I hope my friends ⁹[**will have been exercising** / **will be exercising**] for as many years as I have because I definitely don't want to do this alone!

1B Make it personal Rewrite the paragraph in A beginning with sentence 2, changing "century" to "decade." In pairs, share your hopes for the next ten years.

> When I start my next decade, I hope I …

2A Rewrite the sentences to make them more formal.
1. No doubt your daughter has discovered a solution to peer pressure by now.
2. If we're going to be comfortable economically, we need to save money.
3. I'm sure older people have considered all the options before choosing a nursing home.
4. The government has planned for the fact that pensions are going to be cut back even further by the 2030s.
5. No doubt our planet has been suffering for generations, and we're just paying attention now.

2B Make it personal Choose three sentences from A and make them true. In groups, share opinions.

> No doubt my friend [name] …

3 Change the underlined parts of the responses to cleft or pseudo-cleft sentences. Begin with the word in parentheses.
1. A: I just can't believe Bob didn't throw out the garbage.
   B: <u>The small things always get to you</u>. (it)
2. A: We're not ready to work until we're 75.
   B: That's not a problem. <u>We're not ready for global warming</u>. (it)
3. A: Are you planning to go to grad school?
   B: I'd love to, but <u>I have no idea where I'll get the money</u>. (where)
4. A: Do you ever think about the future?
   B: Sometimes, but <u>I really can't tell you what I'll be doing in 10 years</u>. (what)

> **Bonus!** Language in song
>
> ♪ Wherever you go, whatever you do, I will be right here waiting for you.
>
> Rewrite the song line ending with the words *for fifty years*. What tense did you use?

Grammar expansion

1 More on using the subjunctive (do after 8.2)

In formal speech, the subjunctive can be used with these verbs and expressions.	
Verbs	advise, ask, command, demand, desire, insist, prefer, propose, would rather, recommend, request, suggest, urge
Expressions with *it ... (that)*	It is best, critical, crucial, desirable, essential, imperative, important, preferable, recommended, urgent, vital, a good idea, a bad idea

The subjunctive can also be used in negative, passive, and continuous sentences. Remember that the subjunctive verb is not conjugated and remains in the base form.		
Negative	I suggest	(that) he **not speak** to me in that tone!
Passive	It's critical	(that) he **be fired** immediately.
Continuous	I absolutely insist	(that) you **be waiting** for me when I arrive.

Nevertheless, the subjunctive is limited in English. Do not use it to express the following.		
The future	I'm not leaving	until the manager sees me.
want, would like	I want	you **to refund** my money!
	I'd like (for)	
Emotion	I'm really happy	I **can exchange** this product.
	Sally was angry	the manager **didn't speak** to her yesterday.

In neutral or informal speech, the subjunctive is often avoided.		
Expressions with *it*	It's important	**for** stores **to respect** their customers.
	It's essential	she **expresses** her frustration. (primarily British)
Some verbs	I'd prefer	**for** your staff **to be** a little more polite.
	I recommended	he **should see** the manager. (primarily British)
would rather	I'd rather	you **gave** me the money today!

Common mistakes

I'd like ~~that your manager~~ *(for) your manager to* speak to me now!
I want ~~that she~~ *her to* pay attention.

2 More on adverb clauses with *-ever* words to emphasize conditions (do after 8.4)

Nouns, adjectives, and adverbs may follow *however*. Be careful with count and non-count nouns.			
Non-count noun	However	**much** (money) you spent,	I won't be responsible.
Count noun		**many** times you try to persuade me,	we can't give you a refund.
Adjective		**calm** he may seem,	he's furious inside.
Adverb		**long** you might wait,	we can't see you today.
All of the *-ever* words may express conditions in the past, as well as the present or future. The meaning is sometimes clearest with *may* or *might*.			
Past Continuous	Whichever	one you**'ve chosen** / **may have chosen**,	the purchase is non-refundable.
	Whatever	excuse he**'s given** / **might have given**,	I'm not really interested.

Unit 8

1A Correct the mistakes.
1. On top of that, when I wanted that the waiter apologize, he refused.
2. I suggest your staff to treat me appropriately!
3. I insisted the clerk didn't do that again.
4. The customer took offense when I requested for him to show me the receipt.
5. I demanded my sister gets a refund.
6. I suggest you no use that tone of voice with me ever again!
7. My boss insisted the customer was removed from the store.
8. We were pleased the waiter be understanding when he talked to us.
9. I'll hold on until the owner agree to talk to me.
10. I'd like that this product be replaced right away.

1B Create sentences using the prompts. Which opinions can be expressed using more than one structure?
1. [important / an airline / go / extra mile / customers]
   It's important (that) an airline go the extra mile for customers.
   It's important for an airline to go the extra mile for customers.
2. [I / want / electric company / improve / where I live]
3. [I / rather / stores / not charge / so much / for high-quality merchandise]
4. [add / insult / injury / our government / would like / us / pay / higher / taxes]
5. [everyone / need / take / stand / and demand / restaurant service / improve]
6. [We / demanded / cell-phone service / improve / never / did]

1C Make it personal Make three sentences in B true for you. In pairs, share your opinions.

> Lines at [name of airport] are longer than ever. It's imperative airlines take a stand against inefficiency!

2A Respond to these situations. Begin with an adverb clause, using the words in parentheses.
1. A man calls a store 10 times demanding to speak to the manager.
   Manager to receptionist: _____ (however, times)
2. A woman only wants to buy products she can return, but the store has a "no-returns" policy.
   Sales clerk to woman: _____ (whichever, one)
3. A young man is worried about buying a bed for his overweight father. She reassures him.
   Sales clerk to man: _____ (however, weigh)
4. A polite car salesperson tries to sell a young woman an overpriced car. In the end, she decides against it.
   Woman to salesperson: _____ (however, helpful)

2B Make it personal In pairs, exchange opinions on stores or restaurants near you. Use adverb clauses containing -*ever* words.

> Do you ever go to [name of restaurant]? Service there is pretty good.

> Yeah, well, however polite the waiters may be, the food leaves a lot to be desired.

Bonus! Language in song

♪ It's a bittersweet symphony, this life. Try to make ends meet. You're a slave to the money, then you die.

Which two expressions can be used to combine the last two sentences: *(as) much as*, *however*, or *for all the*? Create two new possible song lines.

Unit 9 — Grammar expansion

1 More on passive expressions in sentences with infinitives (do after 9.2)

More on passive expressions in sentences with infinitives

Acupuncture The treatment It	**is**	reported	to	be	effective. I think I'll try it.
	was			have been	helpful in the past and still is.
	has been	shown		help	patients, including me.
	still hasn't been			have helped	people as much as some people claim.
	might be	thought		be	helpful, but I'm not so sure.
	may have been			have been	out of the mainstream, but it no longer is.

1. If you are unsure what a sentence means, try changing it to an active one.
   Acupuncture **has been reported** to help patients, including me. (passive)
   People **have reported** that acupuncture helps patients. (active)
2. Choose the tense based on the part of the sentence you wish to emphasize. Without additional context, the meaning may be clearer with only one verb in the past. Compare:
   a Acupuncture **was reported** to help patients. (The reporting is in the past. Nothing is said about whether patients are still being helped.)
   b Acupuncture is reported to **have helped** patients. (Patients have been helped in the past up to and including the present. Nothing is said about exactly when the reporting took place.)

Common mistakes

Acupuncture was known to ~~had~~ *have* helped people many years ago.
It was reported to ∧ *have* cured many diseases.

2 More on verb patterns (do after 9.4)

All verb patterns form questions in familiar ways. Only the first verb changes in the formation of the question.

Does your coach	**make** you	**practice** a lot?
What will	**encourage** people	**to lose** weight?
Should teachers	**force** students	**to do** homework?
Has your brother	**appreciated** you	**teaching** him karate?

Passive questions are also very common.

Have you	**been discouraged**	**from going** on a diet?
Will we	**be encouraged**	**to exercise** more?
Should students	**be forced**	**to take** so many exams?
Were you	**made**	**to wear** those ugly shoes as a kid, too?

Common mistakes

Have you been discouraged ~~to try~~ *from trying* hypnotherapy?
Did your teacher make you ~~stayed / to stay~~ *stay* late?

Unit 9

1A Choose the correct meaning below for sentences 1–8.

> 1 Feng Shui <u>was reported</u> long ago to have existed before the invention of the compass.
> 2 It <u>has been known</u> to be effective for thousands of years.
> 3 The 1901 Boxer Rebellion in China <u>was believed</u> to <u>have been caused</u> by Westerners violating principles of Fung Shui during the construction of railroads.
> 4 Feng Shui <u>may have been thought</u> to be a factor, but today the rebellion <u>is known</u> to have had broader causes.
> 5 Feng Shui <u>may be seen</u> to be an Asian custom, but Westerners practice it, too.
> 6 It still <u>hasn't been shown</u> to help people definitively, but it continues to be very popular.
> 7 Many other kinds of alternative medicine <u>have been thought</u> to have developed a long time ago, too.
> 8 They<u>'ve been reported</u> to <u>have been tried</u> in many countries.

1 Historians [**now report / reported earlier**] that the compass was invented before Feng Shui.
2 People [**once knew / still know**] that it is effective.
3 People [**originally believed / believe now**] that Feng Shui caused the Boxer Rebellion.
4 Historians [**no longer think / still think**] Feng Shui caused the rebellion.
5 People [**used to think / still think**] Feng Shui is an Asian custom.
6 Proponents [**once showed / are still trying to show**] that Feng Shui definitely helps people.
7 Historians [**used to think / may still think**] other kinds of alternative medicine are old, too.
8 Doctors [**report / used to report**] they've been tried in many countries.

2A Complete questions 1–5 using the verb patterns on p. 154 and forms of the words in parentheses.

1 A: _____ them recently? (anyone / really / appreciate / you / help)
   B: Yes, my sister has. I helped her move just last week.
2 A: _____ alternative medicine? (people / encourage – passive / try)
   B: I think they should. It's been known to help many!
3 A: _____ anything you didn't want to as a kid? (you / ever / make – passive / do)
   B: I sure was! My mom made me clean up my room every Saturday.
4 A: _____ something new? (you / ever / discourage – passive / try)
   B: Yes, unfortunately. I really wanted to be homeschooled, but my parents were opposed to the idea.
5 A: _____ their wallet to a thief? (anyone you know / ever / force – passive / hand over)
   B: Yes, my mom was held up just a few weeks ago.

2B Make it personal Choose two questions from A to ask a partner. Answer with true information.

> … something new?

> Yes, I wanted to try rock climbing, but everyone said it was dangerous.

Bonus! Language in song

♪ Something in the way you move makes me feel like I can't live without you. It takes me all the way. I want you to stay.

Change the first sentence to a question so you are asking someone about yourself. Be sure to change all the pronouns, too.

155

Grammar expansion

Unit 10

1 More comparative patterns (do after 10.2)

More comparative patterns

My friends are	half	as	important	as	my family (is).
My parents aren't	twice		sympathetic		my friends (are).
I have	three times		**many** friends		Bob (does)
They pay me			**much** attention		Ann (does).
I have	four times	more	money	than	my sister (does).
We have	slightly / far	fewer	friends		we used to (have).
I'm under	much / far / a lot	less	pressure		my friends (are).

Common mistakes

She criticizes me half / twice ~~more~~ *as much as* than my mother.
He has ~~less~~ *fewer* friends than anyone else.

You may say *three times more*, but not *twice more*. *Less* is ungrammatical before a countable noun, even if you may, at times, hear native speakers say it in informal speech.

2 Summary of conditional sentences (do after 10.4)

Inverted conditional sentences are often distinguished from other types of conditional sentences only by register. The sentences below show a sequence from least to most formal.

Present or future meaning	If you change	your mind,	everyone **will be** happy.
			we **would/could give** you a discount.
	If you changed		
	If you were to change		
	Were you to change		
	Should you change		
Past meaning	If I had left	a message,	I'm sure he **would/could have** come.
	Had I left		
	Were I to have left		

Present inversions with *had* and past inversions with *should* are restricted to highly formal or poetic usage:

Had he more money (present), I would marry him.
Should you have had second thoughts (past), I wouldn't have proceeded with the plan.

Unit 10

1A Write sentences with comparative patterns in blue from p. 156 and the information given. There may be more than one answer.

1 My class: 30 students – the other classes: 10 students
   My class has three times as many students as the other classes (do).
   My class has three times more students than the other classes (do).
2 High school grades: important – college grades: double the importance
3 My friends: very understanding – my parents: not very understanding
4 Our cities ten years ago: high unemployment – now: double the unemployment
5 Me: three good friends; my best friend – 15 good friends
6 Your English: very fluent; my English – not as fluent

1B Correct five mistakes in comparative patterns.

A: People have far less friends and less support than they used to because everyone moves around so much.
B: But the good thing about the U.S. is you can make new friends just by joining informal clubs.
A: Yes, but that's hard to do. I had twice more friends before I moved from Washington, D.C. to Los Angeles. And on top of that, now I have to drive such long distances everywhere.
B: It's true. I drive less miles when I want to see friends. But I have half of many as you! I don't know how you do it. Even though you just moved a year ago, you still have twice as much friends as I do!

1C Make it personal Choose two sentences from A. In pairs, share true information.

> Our class has slightly fewer students than the other classes.

> Do you really think so? It seems big to me!

2A Express present or future suggestions or requests informally or formally, according to the cues. Then underline the language in each sentence that shows the register.

1 Mother to child: [clean room / take out for ice cream]
2 Sales clerk to elderly customer: [need help / ask]
3 Employee to boss: [try new approach / double sales]
4 Teenager to younger sister: [not stop that right now / get really mad]
5 Passenger to flight attendant: [have peanuts left over / give me some?]
6 Police officer to driver: [continue to argue / arrest you]

2B Make it personal In pairs, review your sentences in A. Do you agree the register is appropriate?

> OK, number 6: Should you continue to argue, I'll arrest you.

> Police officers are never that formal and polite! I have, "If you continue to argue, I'll arrest you ..."

> Maybe you're right. But it's good for them to be polite in my opinion!

Bonus! Language in song

♪ Where did I go wrong? I lost a friend, Somewhere along in the bitterness. And I would have stayed up with you all night, had I known how to save a life.

Rewrite the inverted conditional sentence using an *if*-conditional clause. Does it refer to present, past, or future time?

2C Change your sentences in A to the past. Which now express a criticism instead of a suggestion or request?

Unit 11 — Grammar expansion

1 More on using modals (do after 11.2)

Modal verbs are very common and fulfill many functions. Below is a summary of common uses. Those with a star haven't been presented earlier in *Identities*.

Possibility	Jim **may / might / could have gone** home early.
Probability	Laura isn't here yet, so she **must be working** late tonight.
Certainty	Laura **couldn't have taken** that train. I saw her on the earlier one.
Obligation	You really **must call** your mother! It's been more than a month!
Advice / Criticism	You **shouldn't have let** so much time go by without talking to her.
Expectation	Fix your flat tire? That **shouldn't be** too hard to do.
Ability	I **could speak** French when I was young, but I **can't speak** it any longer.
Implied *if*-clause	You just found out the airport is closed? I **could have told** you that! (if you'd asked me)
Request	**Could / Can** you **open** the window? It's boiling in here.
*Request / command with annoyance or anger	**Can't** you **sit** still for even for second! **Won't** you just **be** quiet and listen! You can ask questions later. **Would** you **watch** where you're going! You almost ran me over!
Future decision	**I'll pick** you **up** after school. Call me when your class ends.
Refusal	I **won't give** you any more money, no matter how many times you ask.
*Rhetorical question	**Must** I **listen** to that music blaring? I'm trying to concentrate! **Couldn't** you **have** at least **tried** not to spill your coffee? What a mess!
Habitual past action	I used to love to swim, and I **would go swimming** every afternoon.
Permission	Rows 15–30 **may / can** (less formal) now **begin** boarding.
Suggestion	You **might try** doing yoga to help you relax.
Invitation	**Would** you **like** to come to dinner Saturday? We'd love to have you. We're thinking of going to the beach Sunday. **Will** you **join** us?

2 Articles and subject-verb agreement (do after 11.4)

Use of the definite article and whether the verb that follows is singular or plural may differ in some cases from your language. Here are some tips to help you.

Countries: Memorize which countries have articles. All take a singular verb, even if they end in *s*.	The United States has fifty states. The Philippines is a country with numerous islands. Indonesia consists of many islands, too. Peru is famous for Machu Picchu
Collective nouns such as organizations, companies, and stores take a singular verb in American English, and may or may not have an article. Nouns that refer to a category, however, are plural.	The federal government is located in Washington, D.C. Richmond has published *Identities*. Macy's sometimes offers discounts. The fish in that restaurant is very good. (= cooked fish)
	The young take too many risks. Fish are sometimes caught in this bay. (= living fish)
Shared knowledge: Use *the* when you refer to something a second time or the listener knows what you're referring to.	Where are the kids? I don't see them anywhere. I didn't eat the dessert. It didn't look very appetizing.
Fractions may take a singular or plural verb. Expressions involving **time, money,** or **distance** generally require a singular verb.	According to a recent survey, two thirds of adults don't have satisfying jobs, but one third of adults does. 30 miles is a very long way to travel to school! Five dollars is a lot to pay for a soda!

1A Rephrase the underlined sentences with modal verbs. There may be more than one answer.

1. A: Did you hear there was a motorcycle accident this afternoon? I hope it wasn't Ethan.
   B: <u>I'm positive it wasn't</u>. He's always so careful.
   It couldn't have been.
2. A: <u>Stop pointing that umbrella at me</u>! Do you want me to lose an eye?
   B: You don't have to be so nasty about it.
3. A: <u>I expect that Tom is here by now</u>. His plane was due in at 4:00.
   B: Yes, I was just thinking the same thing.
4. A: <u>Aren't you able to talk more quietly</u>? I'm trying to sleep.
   B: Oh, sorry. I didn't realize we were talking loudly.
5. A: Excuse me, is it OK if I turn on my tablet?
   B: Yes. <u>Passengers are now allowed to use portable devices</u>.
6. A: I still haven't run five kilometers in under 30 minutes.
   B: <u>Maybe a good idea is to run more on weekends</u>.
7. A: I'm having Chloe and Alex over for dinner Sunday. <u>I'd like you to come, too</u>.
   B: Oh, I'd love to. Just let me know what to bring.

1B Make it personal Role-play the conversations with a partner. Use modal verbs in the cue sentences.

1. A: (Make a request)
   B: Sure! That shouldn't be too hard to do.
2. A: (Express a possibility)
   B: I could have told you that! I knew all along.
3. A: (Ask a rhetorical question)
   B: You don't have to be so sarcastic. How would I know it was bothering you?
4. A: (Ask permission)
   B: Sure! Go right ahead.
5. A: (Make an angry command)
   B: But we're not! I swear we aren't!
   A: I saw you doing it. Stop it immediately!
6. A: (Make a suggestion)
   B: That's a good idea. I think I'll try it.

2A Correct the mistakes.

1. Steak are a good source of iron.
2. The old is traveling much more now than in the past.
3. They say 25 percent of the young people is unemployed, but everyone I know have a job.
4. The bicycles are usually safe, and bike I have has extra safety features.
5. Japan is the country that have to worry about earthquakes.
6. Ten dollars an hour aren't very much to earn in my opinion!
7. Half of all teenagers has nothing to do after the school.
8. The fruit are important for a balanced diet, but the fruit sold here are never fresh.

2B Make it personal Choose three sentences and start a conversation with a partner. Change them as needed so they are true.

> Fish is a good source of protein, but the frozen fish sold here is tasteless.

> That's a shame. You might want to try cooking fresh fish. It's easy!

> **Bonus! Language in song**
>
> ♪ Oh, I would do anything for love. I would do anything for love, but I won't do that. No, I won't do that.
>
> Which function is expressed in this song line: expectation, a suggestion, refusal, or annoyance? Underline the verb.

159

Grammar expansion

Unit 12

1 More on passive forms with gerunds and infinitives `do after 12.2`

Passive forms with gerunds and infinitives are also common in questions:	
Gerunds …	**Infinitives and base forms …**
1 After certain verbs: **Did** you **like being videoed** by a total stranger?	4 After certain verbs: How **do** you **hope to be remembered**?
2 After prepositions: **Were** you **counting on being** promoted?	5 After adjectives, nouns, and indefinite pronouns: **Is** she the politician most **likely to be elected**?
3 As subjects: Why is **being chosen** important to you?	6 After modals: Why **might** he **be fired**?

After verbs and adjectives, be certain to use the correct prepositions:	
Are you **terrified of** being caught?	Was she **worried about** being fired?
How did you **succeed in** being considered?	Why do your kids **object to** being left alone?
Is she very **discouraged at (by)** not being chosen?	Were you **congratulated on** being elected?

When the question is negative, the meaning may change based on the position of the negative:	
	Meaning
Weren't you **relieved about being fired**? Our boss was a nightmare anyway.	The person *was* fired.
Were you **relieved about** not **being fired**? It's so hard to find a job these days.	The person *wasn't* fired.
Weren't you **hoping to be promoted**? I know you've been here a long time.	The person *wasn't* promoted.
Were you **hoping** not **to be promoted**? You didn't sound happy when they announced it!	The person *was* promoted.

2 More on the *be* and *get* passive `do after 12.4`

The *be* and *get* passives can both be used when talking about actions or something that has changed. But the two passives are not identical and are not always interchangeable.
The *get* passive shows greater informality, emphasis, and negative intent as explained on p. 133:   Get down from there! You could **get hurt**!
Only the *be* passive can be used with stative verbs, such as *say, tell, like*, etc.:   He **was liked** by everyone in the class.   Those criminals **are known**, but the police does nothing about them!
Only the *be* passive is usually used for longer, planned events: The new museum **was opened** in the summer of 2017.   The bridge **was built** to ease the flow of traffic.
The *get* passive is common with verbs like *killed, injured, wounded, paid, hired, fired, laid off*, and *accepted*, which have a clear beneficial or adverse effect on the subject. Neutral verbs, however, generally use the *be* passive: Andy **got / was paid** $1,000 for just two hours of work. BUT   Her shoes **were purchased** at the expensive store down the street.

Unit 12

1A Complete the passive questions using the verbs in parentheses.
1. What school would you like _____ to? (admit)
2. Do you mind _____ to work late? (ask)
3. Do you object more to _____ by your teachers or by your parents? (criticize)
4. How do you want _____ of by people? (think)
5. Are you excited about _____ for the soccer team? (choose)
6. Have you succeeded in _____ for a job you really wanted? (hire)

1B Make it personal Choose two questions to ask a partner. Answer with true information.

> What school would you like to be admitted to?

> Well, I'd really like to go to ... , but tuition has skyrocketed, so I might have to fall back on ...

1C Choose the most logical response in italics (a or b) for conversations 1–4.
1. A: I'm waiting for an acceptance letter to UCLA.
   B: a *Are you scared of not getting in?*
      b *Aren't you scared of getting in?*
   A: No, why would I be?
   B: It's just that I've heard it's a hard school.
2. A: I've been working here for four years now.
   B: a *Are you worried about not being promoted?*
      b *Aren't you worried about being promoted?*
   A: Not really. It would just mean more work if I were.
3. A: I ran into Andrea yesterday.
   B: a *Oh, was she upset at not being invited to the wedding?*
      b *Oh, wasn't she upset at being invited to the wedding?*
   A: I think she was OK with it. This way she doesn't have to buy a gift.
4. A: I'm going to the conference tomorrow.
   B: a *Didn't you mind being asked to give a presentation?*
      b *Did you mind not being asked to give a presentation?*
   A: I was relieved! I don't like speaking in front of lots of people.

2A Change the *get* passive to *be* when it is ungrammatical or unnatural. Check (✔) if it is both correct and natural.
1. My house got broken into last week. They took all my jewelry.
2. I got told that flying cars will have been invented by 2050.
3. I think this shopping center got opened around 10 years ago.
4. The tickets got sold so quickly, we weren't able to buy any.
5. My dad got laid off last month, but luckily he's already found a new job.
6. It's gotten said that global warming is the most serious threat to our planet.

2B In pairs, explain your choices in **A**.

> The first one sounds fine with *get*. It shows emphasis, and it's used to talk about an adverse effect.

2C Make it personal Write three questions to ask a classmate about the future? How long can you continue the conversation?

> **Bonus! Language in song**
>
> ♪ I want to thank you for giving me the best day of my life. Oh just to be with you is having the best day of my life.
>
> Make the song lines negative. In which position does the negative make the most sense?

iDentities

Richmond

WORKBOOK

7.1 What are our most important years?

A ▶27 Listen to a podcast where people share their most important milestones. Choose the correct option (a, b, or c).

 Scott
 Adriana
 Darrell
 Martha

1 What does Scott say about having a baby?
 a It was more important than being ambitious.
 b It was the first time someone else was more important to him than himself.
 c It prevented him from going to college.
2 What was the most difficult thing about the situation Adriana describes?
 a applying for jobs and not getting them
 b working hard
 c accepting the situation
3 What does Darrell say about his life now?
 a He misses working.
 b He does more now than when he was working.
 c He needs to take more control of his situation.
4 Why was it such a shock for Martha to live abroad?
 a People weren't very nice to her.
 b She hadn't realized she'd have to learn a new language.
 c She'd never traveled before.

B ▶27 Listen again. Who says the following things?
 1 It took me a long time to **come to terms with** the situation. _____
 2 ... and I decided I had to **take charge** of my situation. _____
 3 In the end, I really felt like I **came of age** during that time. _____
 4 ... and see how far I'd **gotten off track**. _____
 5 ... all of a sudden **the stakes were higher**. _____
 6 But I **made it through** the hard times. _____

C Match the **bold** expressions in B to meanings 1–6.
 1 reach adulthood _____
 2 take control _____
 3 gone in the wrong direction _____
 4 there's more at risk _____
 5 accept _____
 6 survived _____

D Complete the expressions with these animals.
 1 After years of working in the city, I decided to get out of the _____ race and move to the country.
 2 If I'd known my blog post was going to open such a big can of _____, I'd never have written it.
 3 I'm really sorry, but I think I may have let the _____ out of the bag about your engagement.
 4 I was going to start my own business last year, but I _____ out at the last minute.
 5 Have you heard? Melissa and David are going to have a baby. I heard it straight from the _____ mouth!

E **Make it personal** Describe a situation when you took the bull by the horns.
_____
_____

33

7.2 Would you like to live to be 100?

A Complete the predictions with the future perfect simple or continuous form of the verbs in parentheses.

Who will live to be 100 in 2050? No one knows for sure exactly, but here are some predictions.

Centenarians:
- ¹ _____ (get) married at some time in their lives. 93% of those who live to be 100 today have lived as part of a married couple.
- ² _____ (acknowledge) by their country. In the UK, centenarians receive a telegram from the queen. In Ireland, they receive a "Centenarian Bounty" of €2,540, and in Japan, they receive a silver cup and a letter.
- ³ _____ (have) children later in life. Woman who have had children in their 40s are four times as likely to live to 100.
- ⁴ _____ (exercise) every day for many years. They also ⁵ _____ (not be) overweight.
- ⁶ _____ (live) most of their lives in France or Japan. Statistics show that these two countries produce the highest number of centenarians.

B Correct the mistakes in these sentences. One sentence is correct.
1 By the time they retire, the average American will have been earned 1.4 million dollars.
2 I will have been traveling to over 50 countries by the time I'm 70.
3 Statistics show that 40% of the workplace will have been forced into early retirement through illness.
4 The new retirement laws won't have been coming into effect by the time she retires.
5 Next year, Bill will have been worked for 50 years, and he shows no signs of wanting to stop yet!
6 By 2025, it's expected that more money will have allocated to services for the elderly.

C ▶ 28 Circle the correct options. Listen to check.
1 A: How long has Rita been with us?
   B: At the end of the year, she *will have been working / will have been worked* here for 30 years.
   A: Really? We should get her a present or something.
2 A: Do you think you'll still be working in 10 years?
   B: I hope not! I *will have been retired / will have retired* by then if I have enough money saved.
3 A: Have you heard the news about the job layoffs?
   B: Again? That means that by the end of the year, more than 2,000 people *will have been fired / will have fired*!
   A: I know, either that, or they *will be forced / will have been forced* into early retirement.
4 A: We *will have saved / will have been saving* $5,000 by the end of the year.
   B: Really? We should do something nice to celebrate.
5 A: It says here that by the end of the financial crisis, more than twenty thousand people *will have been losing / will have lost* their jobs.
   B: Oh, that's sad.

D Make it personal Rewrite the sentences so they're true for you.
1 I will have retired by the time I'm 50.
   _____
2 When I'm 90, I will have been working all my life.
   _____

Do babies ever surprise you? 7.3

A Read the article. Does the writer think we are born honest or dishonest?

Are we born HONEST?

A Aw, look at that sweet, innocent face. Fresh to the world, and as yet not corrupted by the evils of the world around them, it's difficult to believe that babies are capable of anything other than honesty. Surely they don't even have the mental capacity at that age to lie? Well, if recent research is anything to go by, it appears that may not be true.

B Until now, there has been a general consensus that we are born honest, and it's not until we come into contact with the wider world that we develop the ability to bend the truth. What's more, we don't develop the language or [1]_____ expressions needed in order to lie until the age of four. Lying is a complex cognitive procedure, an [2]_____ decision based on the experience we gain in our [3]_____ lives, with which we need to have an understanding of what's right or wrong.

C Current research, however, has blown that idea out of the water. It seems lying is an [4]_____ trait. A recent study showed that babies as young as six months old use fake crying and pretend laughing to get what they want. Lying is actually a [5]_____ ability babies develop in the [6]_____ stages of life. A [7]_____ sense of what's right and wrong, it appears, doesn't come until later in childhood. This is why fairy tales and children's stories with a moral are so important.

D What's more, babies don't just lie, but go as far as to manipulate to get what they want. They'll scream, hit themselves, and even hold their breath until they pass out – a condition known as a "breath-holding spell." This might seem like an [8]_____ transaction, but to babies, it's a [9]_____ deal. If they want it, why can't they have it?

E All of this seems to point towards the conclusion that humans are inherently born dishonest. Rather than shield children from the reality of life to prevent them from being "corrupted," it's, therefore, more important to educate them from an early age as to what's right and what's wrong.

B Match summary sentences 1–6 to paragraphs A–E. There's one extra sentence.
1 ☐ Babies are actually capable of lying.
2 ☐ Babies will even do more than just lie to achieve things.
3 ☐ We think babies are born honest and later develop the ability to lie.
4 ☐ Babies don't actually know how to be honest.
5 ☐ It's important to teach young children a sense of morality.
6 ☐ Babies look honest and unable to lie.

C Complete the collocations in the article with these adjectives.

| crucial   daily   early   evolutionary   fair   facial   informed   rudimentary   unfair |

7.4 Do you seem younger or older than you are?

A Order the words in italics to complete the cleft sentences in the text.

Achieving the impossible

¹*not / that / are / old / you / it's / how* determines what you are able to achieve. And these people have proved it. Take Teiichi Igarashi, for example. At the ripe old age of 100, he became the first centenarian to climb Mount Fuji in Japan. ²*time / it / the / wasn't / that / first* he'd done it, either. It was his 12th ascent!

³*people / who / just / not / it's / young* can set world records, either. In May 2016, ⁴*100 year-old / who / was / Ida Keeling / it* set a new world record of 1:17:33 in the 60-meter dash for U.S. women over age 90.

Some people say you can't teach an old dog new tricks, but the case of Nola Ochs goes to show that ⁵*age / your / it's / that / not* stops you from learning. At 95, she became the oldest person to attain a college degree. As if that wasn't remarkable enough, at 98 she went on to graduate with a Master's degree!

It just goes to show that time is no obstacle to what we can achieve when we really apply ourselves. ⁶*yourself / it's / that / belief / in / only / your* holds you back, not your age.

Ida Keeling

Nola Ochs

1 _____
2 _____
3 _____
4 _____
5 _____
6 _____

B Rewrite these people's opinions on the article using a cleft sentence.

1 "I only feel respect when I see people's achievements."
 It's _____ when I see their achievements.

2 "Your attitude determines what you can do – at any age."
 It's _____ what you can do – at any age.

3 "I'm most impressed by their perspective on life."
 It's _____ impresses me most.

4 "These people have a belief in themselves."
 It's _____ these people have.

5 "Their achievements leave me speechless."
 It's _____ me speechless.

C ▶29 Complete the text with these words. Listen to check.

| act conform hand heart pushing wise |

Everyone tells me I should ¹_____ my age, but why should I? OK, I'm ²_____ 90, but that doesn't mean I should ³_____ to expectations. I want to make the most of the time I have left, and I want to gain first-⁴_____ experience in all the things I've always dreamed about. When I was younger, I was far too practical, you see. People said I was "⁵_____ beyond my years" but, to tell you the truth, I wish I'd been a bit more adventurous, made a few more mistakes. Well, I might be old now, but I'm young at ⁶_____ , and if it keeps me healthy and fit, then all the better!

D **Make it personal** Complete the sentences so they're true for you.

1 It was my parents who _____ .
2 It's _____ that impresses me most.

What would your ideal job be? 7.5

A Read the job-application letter. Which of the following does James not have a lot of?

☐ qualifications   ☐ experience   ☐ skills

Director of Studies —•— Fast track English   September 30

Dear Sir or Madam,

I am writing in ¹_____ to your job opening for an English teacher, as advertised online on September 24. I believe I am highly ²_____ to the position, and am attaching a recent copy of my résumé.

Having graduated last year with a Master's in Linguistics, I am eager to find full-time employment as an English teacher. As you will ³_____ on my résumé, a large part of my degree consisted of practice teaching, for which I achieved high ratings. I, therefore, believe my knowledge and experience to date would be a perfect ⁴_____ for the position you have available.

While teaching as part of my graduate program, I was told by my professors that I have a dynamic presence in the classroom, and I am attentive to my students' needs. I communicate well, and I believe I am receptive to new ideas. I am also proactive in helping students reach their full potential. Before starting college, I worked part-time as a receptionist at a small private language school. My responsibilities there included registering new students, answering questions, and maintaining up-to-date records. In this ⁵_____ , I was also able to gain valuable insights into the running of a school.

While I am aware my teaching experience is not yet extensive, I am no stranger to the classroom. I am also responsive to feedback and have a good knowledge of teaching theory, which I believe I will be able to convert into practical day-to-day teaching solutions.

I hope you will give my application careful ⁶_____ . Thank you very much in advance.
Sincerely,

James Tuffnal

James Tuffnal

B Complete the letter with these words. There's one extra.

capacity   consideration   fit   response   responsibility   see   suited

C Match the highlighted words in the letter to definitions 1–4.

1 ready to accept new suggestions _____
2 wants to create solutions _____
3 able to pay close attention _____
4 energetic and exciting _____

D Circle the correct option.

1 I wonder if I could *possibly / probably* borrow your tablet for an hour or so.
2 **A:** I hope I'm not *disturbing / interrupting*.
   B: No, it's fine. How can I help you?
3 Ah, Michael. Come in. Would you be so *kind / lovely* as to close the door?
4 I had an idea for the marketing campaign that I wanted to *run / walk* by you.
5 **A:** So that's my idea for the budget. *Would / Should* it be OK if I went ahead?
   B: I'll need to check some of those numbers, but I think they'll be OK.

E Look back at lessons 7.1–7.5 in the Student's Book. Find the connection between the song lines and the content of each lesson.

F ▶30 Listen to the five question titles from the unit, and record your answers to them. If possible, compare recordings with a classmate.

37

8 » 8.1 What makes a restaurant special?

A ▶31 Listen to a radio interview with Cameron Mathis from the Movement Against Patronizing Advertisements (MAPA). Which four things does he not like to see in advertising?

1. ☐ images used to represent a company or product in a childish way
2. ☐ online ads
3. ☐ people with childish faces
4. ☐ commercials aimed at children
5. ☐ childish music
6. ☐ false claims about products

B ▶31 Listen again. True (T) or false (F)?

1. MAPA is against all advertising.
2. Cameron thinks some ads could be mistaken for children's programs.
3. He thinks childish ads make people less critical.
4. He thinks children should be involved in making decisions about paying bills.
5. MAPA wants to take these companies to court.
6. He believes we all have to protest against this type of advertising.

C Match phrases 1–5 from the listening to what they refer to (a–e). One matches to two items.

1. taking the Internet by storm
2. take a stand against
3. take offense at
4. take the blame for
5. take matters into their own hands

a. ☐ commercials that treat us like children
b. ☐ companies that use childish advertising
c. ☐ good ads
d. ☐ people in general (what they need to do)
e. ☐ the "dumbing-down" of society

D Complete the conversations with these words. There's one extra.

> apologize   enough   insult   matters   top

1. **A:** Oh, I hate this ad!
   B: Me too! And to make _____ worse, it's on all the time!
2. **A:** Have you seen that commercial for orange juice?
   B: No, why?
   A: It's awful. They have this little singing band of oranges. On _____ of that, they all shouted "Juiced!" at the end, in these really childish voices.
3. **A:** I'm not sure I liked Neil's idea for our new poster campaign.
   B: I know, right? Absolutely terrible. As if that were not _____ , I think the boss actually liked it.
4. **A:** I'm thinking about going to that new Italian restaurant advertised in the local paper.
   B: I wouldn't if I were you. We went there last week. The service was terrible, and our food was cold when it arrived. To add _____ to injury, they charged us extra for water!

E Make it personal Answer the questions.

1. What types of things do you take offense at? _____
2. When did you last take a stand against something? _____
3. In what situations would you take matters into your own hands? _____
4. Describe something that is currently taking the Internet by storm. _____

Are you a demanding customer? 8.2

A Circle the correct option in the complaints.

Five ridiculous customer complaints that will make you laugh

1 Visitors to a zoo were disappointed when the animals looked sad. They insisted the zookeepers *make / to make* the animals smile.

2 After going on a hot-air balloon trip and feeling utterly terrified, one customer said it was essential *for / that* the organizers display a sign to warn people they shouldn't get on if they're afraid of heights.

3 One visitor to Disneyland demanded the company *to refund / refund* his ticket after complaining it was "too touristy."

4 A movie-goer, after watching Titanic, complained online that she wished the story *weren't / aren't* so predictable.

5 A vacationer in Greece suggested a resort *looks / look* into its discriminatory policies after reading a sign which said "No hairdressers on site." She felt discriminated against because she was a hairdresser.

B Rewrite the sentences to make them more formal. Use the subjunctive.

1 You need to listen to your customers. It's important _____ .
2 I want your company to give me a refund! I insist _____ .
3 You really must make customers aware of your policy first. It's essential _____ .
4 I'm sad this dress is so expensive. I wish _____ .
5 You should be more polite when taking orders. I suggest _____ .
6 I want you to give me a bigger seat! I demand _____ .

C ▶32 Complete the text with the correct subjunctive form of these verbs. Listen to check.

| be   give   not be   know   reassess   write |

👎 How to complain effectively 👎

Some people are very good at complaining when they receive bad service and know exactly how to get what they want in terms of compensation. Here's what to do.

Firstly, it's essential you ¹_____ what you want to achieve. If you're going into a complaint without knowing what action you want taken, then I suggest you ²_____ what it is you're looking for.

When you complain, it's important you ³_____ or go in person. Don't use the phone, as it's unlikely you'll be put through to the right person. Also, the company can hang up. If a visit doesn't work, try social media. Most companies today secretly wish social media ⁴_____ in existence, as it's an effective way to voice your complaint to the world.

It's critical that you ⁵_____ polite at all times. This will ensure the other person is on your side and will want to help you – and that's half the battle.

Finally, don't make ridiculous demands such as "I insist you ⁶_____ me a free vacation." Give the company something to work with, and it's more likely to find an acceptable solution.

D Make it personal Complete the sentences so they're true for you.

1 I wish most companies _____ .
2 If I receive bad service, I insist _____ .
3 When complaining, I think it's essential _____ .

39

8.3 What are the worst aspects of air travel?

A Read and complete the article with headings a–e. There's one extra.

a It's not a bed!
b Don't hog the space!
c Take it with you when you leave!
d Be quiet!
e Keep your shoes on!

Nightmare passengers

All too often we hear complaints about airlines – delayed flights, not enough legroom, and poor-quality food – we wish it weren't like this, but it's the reality of air travel today. The fact that most airlines in recent years have gone to great lengths to cut costs hasn't really helped matters, either. But is it just passengers who suffer? We took it upon ourselves to interview 100 airline employees to find out what their biggest gripes are.

1 ☐ Most everyone we spoke to complained about passengers who exposed their bare – and often smelly – feet. One flight attendant told us about a passenger who went the extra mile in order to get comfortable by poking his feet in the space between the two seats in front – while everyone was eating! The people in front got a nasty shock, and luckily Judy, a seasoned flight attendant, was there and saw to it that he stopped. "It's not uncommon to see feet in the air, on tables, in the aisles," says Judy. "People will move mountains to give their dirty feet an airing."

2 ☐ Some people simply refuse to put their small bags under the seat in front. "This happens at least once every flight," said Michael, a flight attendant for a leading American airline. "We have to explain that they take up valuable overhead space, and that it's essential we leave it free for bigger bags. However, more often than not, the customer will insist on leaving the bag there, even after we go out of our way to find a better place for it."

3 ☐ "You wouldn't believe what people leave behind," continues Michael, when we ask him about messy travelers. From chewing gum, to dirty diapers! Some people seem to treat the plane as a giant, flying trash can, leaving the exhausted flight attendants to clean up after them.

4 ☐ While these examples aren't a direct problem for airline staff, they cause a lot of aggravation. While most of us accept the need for a little comfort on a long-haul flight, there are some passengers who feel that even for a short, thirty-minute hop, it's acceptable to slam their seat back straight after takeoff. Worse still, the passenger sitting behind might take it from there and purposely kick the other passenger's seat, causing arguments and sometimes violence, which you really don't want when you're at 15,000 feet.

B Circle the correct option to complete the sentences about the article.
1 Cheaper air fares have made problems for passengers *better / worse*.
2 One passenger exposed his feet to others during *meal time / takeoff*.
3 People put small bags in the overhead compartment even when *there isn't space / the flight attendant asks them not to*.
4 Some people leave *used baby products / drinks* on their seats when they leave.
5 The writer believe it's *unacceptable / acceptable* to recline your seat on a flight with a long duration.

C Complete the statements with a word from the article.
1 Even though our seats were booked separately, the flight attendant went to great _____ to ensure we could sit together.
2 The guy sitting next to me took it _____ himself to offer me his vegetarian meal.
3 The flight attendant _____ to it that I had enough space for my bag in the overhead compartment.
4 The woman sitting next me went out of her _____ to make sure she had full use of the arm rest!
5 After showing you to the gate, the airline staff will _____ it from there and guide you onto the airplane.

40

Have you ever borrowed money? 8.4

A Complete the text with these words and phrases.

> as useful as   for all the   however   much as   whatever

Avoid sorrow when you borrow

If you're thinking of borrowing money, it's important you do so wisely in order to avoid falling into the debt trap. ¹_____ amazing offers banks and credit companies provide, repaying the loan should always be your most important consideration.

- First of all, know the terms. ²_____ the deal may be, always, always read the small print. If it's a credit card, are there any annual fees? If it's a loan, and it's interest-free for the first six months, what will the interest be after that? ³_____ attractive the money may seem at first, is your financial situation really likely to improve after that time?

- Secondly, seek advice from an independent source. ⁴_____ loan companies might be when "selling" you the loan, they want you to borrow from them at the end of the day. There are numerous places that offer free advice, both online and in person. Run the terms by them first.

- Finally, do your math. ⁵_____ a $50 monthly repayment appears manageable, work out how much you'll end up repaying in total. It might not look so attractive after all.

B Match 1–5 to endings a–e to make sentences.

1 For all the help the bank
2 As useful as credit cards
3 Whatever interest rate they
4 However helpful the bank
5 As much as you

a ☐ might be, you still need to get independent advice, too.
b ☐ may be, it's important you keep track of how much you spend.
c ☐ want to borrow the money, make sure you can really afford it.
d ☐ offers, it just wants your money.
e ☐ might offer, you'll still pay back a lot more than you borrowed.

C Use the clues to complete the crossword with words related to money.

ACROSS

1 Business was good last year. We made a _____ of $120,000.
3 Can you believe that café? They wanted to _____ me $25 for a sandwich!
5 I need to _____ some money so I can buy a new car.
6 A: But I thought it was cheaper than that?
   B: The price doesn't include _____ .

DOWN

2 I've just heard that I'm going to _____ money from a long-lost relative.
4 We can offer you a _____ with an interest rate of 18%.

41

8.5 What was the last complaint you made?

A Read the letter of complaint and choose the correct summary.

1 The family's bags were damaged.
2 The family's bags were lost.
3 The family's bags arrived late.

Mr. Paul Gaines
Customer Service Director

Dear Mr. Gaines:

I am writing with reference to a recent experience I had when flying on your airline from San José del Cabo to Los Angeles. I have already spoken to your customer-service representatives to try and ¹*rectify / reason* the problem by phone, but to no ²*answer / avail*.

On December 24 last year, I traveled with my family to San José del Cabo, for our annual vacation. We were supposed to connect in Phoenix, Arizona with a two-hour layover, but when we arrived at LAX airport for our flight, we were told that our flight had been delayed by three hours, and that we would make a later connection to Mexico. We were also told that our baggage would arrive safely on the later flight. Notwithstanding the ³*information / fact* that we were given this assurance by your ground crew, when we arrived in San José del Cabo, our luggage was not there. When I spoke to staff in the airport to try to ⁴*repeat / resolve* the issue, I was told that it would be delivered the next morning to our hotel.

However, it actually took ten days to arrive because it had been left at the airport for most of that time. I would have been ⁵*happy / delighted* to come and collect it, but your staff told me on the phone repeatedly that this was not company policy. As I'm sure you can appreciate, this ruined our vacation, which we spent primarily shopping for new clothes.

While I understand that this is a busy time of year for you, especially at this destination, this level of service is nonetheless unacceptable. I trust that you will seek to reimburse me for the extra expenses I incurred. In the event that I do not receive ⁶*satisfaction / money*, I will have no choice but to consider ⁷*law / legal* action. I hope these ⁸*stairs / steps* will not be necessary.

I thank you in advance for your attention to this matter. I look ⁹*after / forward* to a response.

Sincerely yours,
Lily Weston

B Circle the correct options to complete the letter.

C Replace the underlined words in the sentences with more formal alternatives.

1 I have called you repeatedly, but to no <u>success</u>. _____
2 I hope you are able to <u>help</u> me. _____
3 I look forward to <u>an answer</u>. _____
4 <u>In spite of</u> the fact that they assured me they would call me back, they didn't. _____
5 I trust you will <u>correct</u> the matter as soon as possible. _____

D Look back at lessons 8.1–8.5 in the Student's Book. Find the connection between the song lines and the content of each lesson.

E ▶ 33 Listen to the five question titles from the unit, and record your answers to them. If possible, compare recordings with a classmate.

9.1 Would you like to be a teacher?

A Read the definition of mindfulness and choose the best summary.
1. ☐ It doesn't make our problems go away, but helps us not get stressed out by them.
2. ☐ It helps us forget about our problems and focus on what's good in our lives.
3. ☐ It doesn't make our problems go away, and it can be harmful.

what is mindfulness?

Mindfulness is a way of silently focusing the mind on what we feel and what we do in our lives, in order to achieve calmness and greater clarity in the way we think. It is not intended to stop us from feeling life's pressures, but it does help us be conscious of them and cope with them in a calm, relaxed manner

B ▶34 Listen to a news story about mindfulness training at school. Match the people (1–4) with the comments about them (a–d).

1. The government
2. Grangeville Elementary
3. Some parents
4. Dorothy Quinn and the teachers

a. ☐ They weren't convinced the program was a good idea at first.
b. ☐ They have introduced regular mindfulness training.
c. ☐ They knew the program would be beneficial from the start.
d. ☐ They want to introduce regular mindfulness training.

C ▶34 Listen again and choose the correct answer (a, b, or c). Are you convinced by mindfulness?

1. Research has shown mindfulness training to have benefits for children …
   a only during class time.   b both inside and outside school.   c only on exams.
2. At first, the training was for …
   a all students.   b teachers.   c some students.
3. In a mindfulness class …
   a students do different physical activities.   b do intelligence tests.   c breathe deeply.
4. The number of children at Grangeville Elementary doing the training has …
   a grown.   b fallen.   c stayed the same.
5. The school has replaced _____ with mindfulness training.
   a physical education   b some disciplinary measures   c some subjects

D ▶35 Complete the extracts with verbs beginning with *out*. Listen to check.

1. We felt the benefits would _____ the time factor.
2. The children in the program consistently _____ those who opted out.
3. More and more children joined the program, and they now _____ considerably those who didn't take part.
4. We're also finding that their concentration levels _____ the others, too.
5. These kids _____ their immature behavior much more quickly.
6. Rather than trying to _____ the teachers and break the rules, they're being much more cooperative.

E **Make it personal** Change the sentences so they're true for you.

1. I think the benefits of traditional education outweigh those of trying new approaches.
2. There were some school subjects in which I outperformed my classmates.

9.2 What is alternative medicine?

A Use the prompts (1–7) to complete the passive expressions. Any surprises?

Medical myths

- "Immune boosters" ¹[believe / help / you] _are believed to help you_ get over a cold or flu. But actually, the bad effects you feel when you have a cold or flu – sneezing, coughing, runny nose – are signs that your immune system is working just fine. Any perceived "boost" to these ²[can / expect / make / you] _____ feel worse.

- Another cold and flu fallacy is that vitamin C ³[know / be / effective] _____ in treating them, right? Not so. In fact, there have been no conclusive studies to show that it works.

- Other supplements, such as multivitamin pills, ⁴[think / be / good] _____ for you, too. However, recent studies show that they are largely ineffectual. And because the supplement industry is largely unregulated, there have been no major studies into their safety.

- Drinking eight glasses of water a day ⁵[believe / hydrate / your body] _____ sufficiently. But this is based on very old medical advice, and nowadays water ⁶[known / come from / other sources] _____ , such as food. We're not walking around in a constant state of dehydration.

- For a long time in the past, sugar ⁷[report / make / kids] _____ hyperactive. But this is also not based on any conclusive studies.

B Complete the second sentence so that it has the same meaning as the first. Use passive expressions with infinitives.

1 They report that the treatments are successful.
  The treatments _____ .
2 We think that humans use only 10% of their brains.
  Humans _____ only 10% of their brains.
3 They believe that the new drug may be a miracle cure.
  The new drug _____ a miracle cure.
4 But, in fact, we know it doesn't work.
  But, in fact, it _____ .

C ▶36 Choose a word from each box A–C in the correct form to complete the conversation with three-word phrasal verbs. Listen to check.

A	B	C
come give go grow watch	down out (x2) through up	of for on with (x2)

TODD: What's wrong, Becky? You don't look well.
BECKY: Ugh, I think I'm ¹_____ a cold. The problem is it usually makes my asthma worse, too.
TODD: Oh, that's awful. I used to have asthma when I was a child, but I ²_____ it as I got older. Have you tried any alternative therapies?
BECKY: Oh, I've been ³_____ alternative therapies for ages now. I tried acupuncture a while back, and I went a few times, but didn't manage to ⁴_____ the total number of recommended sessions.
TODD: Yes, I know what you mean. I've tried herbal remedies for other things, but they never really worked, so I just ⁵_____ them.

D Make it personal Complete the sentences to express your own opinions.

1 Traditional medicine is believed _____ .
2 Alternative medicine is thought _____ .

What unconventional families do you know? 9.3

A Read the introduction to the article. Which sentence (1–3) best reflects the author's opinion?
1. ☐ Happy couples never fight.
2. ☐ People need to be realistic about making a long-term relationship work.
3. ☐ If you find the right person, it's easy to be happy for a long time.

What's the secret to a successful marriage?

Long-term relationships are hard work, but if you go about them in the right way, they can mean long-lasting happiness. Obviously no one expects a fairytale [1]_____, but some people are able to make it work over time. We spoke to four of those people and asked them for their best tips.

I think it's important to have a common interest and do things together. While you shouldn't have to compromise your own interests, it's good to have some you share, too. This will ensure that you spend time together, and, in the end, you'll have an overriding [2]_____ to do this *with* your partner, not *without*. **Mike, 56**

It sounds obvious, but what works most for us is being open and honest. I think a lot of people have this fictitious [3]_____ that if there's something bothering them, then they shouldn't trouble their significant other with it. But bottled up feelings can grow into resentment – and then you're in treacherous territory. So, if something worries you, tell him or her. You don't have to always have a lengthy [4]_____ about it, but getting it out in the open means you can deal with it more easily and move on. **Celia, 33**

Successful couples are thought to lead happy lives, without any major crises, but that's just not true. Everyone has problems, but what's important is how you deal with them. The key is to approach problems together and in different ways. If you always do the same thing, then you'll always have the same problems. Don't make unilateral [5]_____ – discuss the best way to solve things together. You'll find your partner becomes a valuable security [6]_____ in times of trouble. **Darren, 38**

I know it's easy to say this, but when you're looking for a prospective [7]_____, don't settle for anyone who treats you as anything less than special. Before I met my hubby, I dated a few guys who were wonderful at first, but, after a while, started to criticize me rather than just love me for who I am. In those early days, watch how they treat other people – their parents, salesclerks, coworkers. That will show you how they'll treat you in years to come. If they're not kind, then they're not up to the task of being your life companion, let alone child [8]_____. **Angela, 28**

B Read the rest of the article, ignoring the blanks. Match the possible situations 1–4 to each person.
1. They were having financial problems, so decided to sell their car and use public transportation to get to work instead. _____
2. Both members of this couple have their own set of friends, but on Sundays they're going biking in the park together. _____
3. She wanted to go back to college to get a degree. He told her he thought she'd do really well. _____
4. He was worried that she was spending a lot of time with a coworker. He spoke to her about it, and she told him they were just working on a project together for six weeks. _____

C Re-read the article. True (T) or false (F)? Whose advice did you think was best?
1. Mike thinks it's difficult to find time to do things together.
2. Celia doesn't like to trouble her partner with small things that worry her.
3. She thinks you don't have to spend a lot of time talking about how you feel.
4. Darren thinks relationships can be difficult, and you should find a way of solving problems by yourself.
5. Angela thinks some partners might treat you differently over time.

D Complete the article with these words.

| belief | blanket | choices | discussion | desire | ending | mate | rearing |

45

9.4 How often do you work out?

A Circle the correct options.

Pablo's story

Two years ago, I was horrendously overweight, eating badly, and feeling depressed. My doctor urged me ¹*to change / change* my lifestyle, but I had no idea where to start. My weight prevented me ²*to do / from doing* anything too strenuous, such as running, but I knew I had to do something. So I went to see a nutritionist, and she had me ³*to make / make* small changes to my diet. For example, she encouraged me ⁴*to replace / from replacing* all chocolate and candy with fruit. It was hard at first, but I insisted ⁵*to keep / on keeping* at it, and gradually, I started to actually enjoy it. Eventually, the weight started coming off, and this enabled me ⁶*to start / starting* exercising. I joined a gym, and there I had a personal trainer who was great. He warned me ⁷*to do / not to do* too much, too quickly at first. But at the same time, he made me ⁸*do / to do* exercises I wouldn't have thought of doing otherwise. I really appreciated ⁹*his / he* helping me patiently like that. Since then, I've lost nearly 50 pounds, and it's helped me ¹⁰*enjoy / enjoying* life so much more.

B Correct the mistake in these sentences. One sentence is correct.
1 When I was younger, my parents dissuaded me eating too much candy. _____
2 My leg injury caused me stopping running for two months. _____
3 The gym won't let you to join until you've had a checkup with your doctor. _____
4 Schools should discourage children to eat junk food. _____
5 This new app reminds you to do exercise throughout the day. _____
6 My personal trainer discouraged me from lift too much weight at first. _____

C Complete the text with the verb form of the words in parentheses.

There's no denying that living a sedimentary lifestyle can ¹_____ (threat) our health in many different ways. Sitting at a desk all day can not only ²_____ (weak) our muscles, but also ³_____ (worse) our health in other ways, such as giving us bad posture. The problem is, with a busy work schedule, many of us just don't have the time to visit the gym every day. But you don't need to join an expensive gym in order to stay in shape and remain healthy. There are many different exercises you can do at home or at work, using only your body weight. You can ⁴_____ (soft) the blow by doing them in short intervals, spread throughout the day. And as you become more adept, there's no need to ⁵_____ (length) each workout either, but just do more intervals. You really can ⁶_____ (strength) your body this way, and, not only this, it will ⁷_____ (fresh) you up so you can stay more alert and focused while working.

Visit **deskworkouts.id** for more details about our training schedules.

No time for the gym? No problem!

D Make it personal Complete the sentences so they're true for you.
1 When I was young, my parents always encouraged me _____ .
2 I'd love to have someone _____ .
3 I wish someone had dissuaded me _____ .

What are the pros and cons of dieting? 9.5

A Read the report. Is the writer for or against dieting overall?

A report on the pros and cons of dieting

Today's image-obsessed society puts a lot of pressure on people to lose weight and aim for a slender physique. Added to this, obesity levels have been steadily rising in many developed countries to unhealthy proportions. For these reasons, many people attempt to lose weight by dieting, following carefully-controlled plans that aim to limit the amount of calories they consume each day. There are many reasons given for doing this.

- ^{1}_____: Simply put, if you consume fewer calories than you use each day, you'll lose weight. Restricting the number of calories you consume by following a diet plan will enable you to do this.
- ^{2}_____: As you begin to shed the pounds, you'll feel better about yourself and the way you look.
- ^{3}_____: Focusing on what you put in your body every day makes you notice what you eat more, and avoid subconsciously eating when perhaps you don't really need to.
- ^{4}_____: A diet plan helps you learn about what types of food contain more calories and increase your cholesterol, as well as which foods provide healthier alternatives.

Nevertheless, there are just as many reasons why following a carefully controlled diet to lose weight can be harmful. Following a strict diet can ...

- ^{5}_____ only a short-term solution, which may even cause you to put more weight back on after you've achieved your "target weight."
- ^{6}_____ to muscle loss, as your body looks for the energy it needs elsewhere.
- ^{7}_____ an unhealthy relationship with food, as you begin to worry about everything you eat.
- ^{8}_____ your metabolism, causing your body to actually store more food as fat than use it for energy.

While there are clear benefits to dieting for weight loss, changing your lifestyle and exercising regularly will be easier to maintain over time. It will also generally make you much healthier.

B Complete the report with these nouns and verbs.

Nouns: awareness   confidence   education   weight loss

Verbs: create   lead   provide   slow

C Rewrite each list from a report with a consistent style.

| 1 Doing regular exercise can help you ...
• strengthen your heart.
• weight loss.
• keep alert and focused. | 2 There are many reasons people join a gym.
• Motivation: Getting there encourages you to actually exercise.
• Equipment: You can use state-of-the-art equipment you don't have at home.
• Provide a safe environment: You are monitored and trained to exercise safely. | 3 People who regularly practice mindfulness ...
• concentration at work better.
• are generally more relaxed.
• feel better able to deal with life's pressures. |

D Circle the correct option.

1 Did I hear you *correctly / rightly*? You're on a raw-food, vegan diet?
2 Who in their right *brain / mind* would count all the calories they eat every day?
3 **A:** Gary really needs to do more exercise. He's really overweight.
   B: You should reserve *judging / judgment*. You're not so healthy yourself.

E Look back at lessons 9.1–9.5 in the Student's Book. Find the connection between the song lines and the content of each lesson.

F ▶ 37 Listen to the five question titles from the unit, and record your answers to them. If possible, compare recordings with a classmate.

10 » 10.1   Why do friends drift apart?

A ▶38 Listen to Ron telling his girlfriend Eva about a friend he once had and answer the questions.
1 What was gone from Ron's house?
2 What did James do after that?

B ▶38 Listen again. Complete 1–6 with *Ron* or *James*.
1 _____ doesn't think he was a real friend.
2 _____ made his life more interesting when he arrived.
3 _____ began behaving badly towards him.
4 _____ went out of the room suddenly.
5 _____ found a new group of friends.
6 _____ felt like he had been deceived.

C ▶39 Listen to Eva describe a time she lost her friend, Judy. What do these words refer to?
1 five *They'd been friends since they were five.*
2 the need to speak _____
3 early twenties _____
4 calls _____
5 Illinois _____

D Match 1–7 to a–g to form extracts from the listening.
1 He was a breath
2 The life
3 Oh, what a
4 We went
5 Real birds
6 Our conversations always went
7 I mean, we didn't always

a ☐ of the party, you know?
b ☐ beneath the surface.
c ☐ of fresh air.
d ☐ see eye to eye …
e ☐ back a long way.
f ☐ riot he was!
g ☐ of a feather.

E Circle the correct options.

1 Do you get along with Bobby?

   Not really. There's no *saying / telling* why. We've just never really hit it off.

2 Can you call Chrissie for me?

   Easier *said / told* than done! She never picks up her phone.

3 Why didn't you keep in touch with Charlotte?

   Truth be *said / told*, I never really wanted to.

4 I guess it goes without *saying / telling* you'll be inviting Will to your party.

   Of course!

5 *Say / Tell* what you will about Beth, she's always been there for you.

   You're right. She's a great friend.

48

Who's the oldest person you know? 10.2

A Complete the article with these words. There's one extra.

> bit every bit far hardly quite near the harder whole

Making friends in old age

The older you get, ¹_____ it is to make friends. When you retire, you spend less time at work and so feel a ²_____ lot more isolated than when you were working. In reality, though, you're nowhere ³_____ as isolated as you think. There are literally thousands of other people your age who are ⁴_____ as eager to make friends as you are. And making new friends isn't ⁵_____ as difficult as you think.

Often people think that they should join clubs or take up a new hobby just to make friends. But it's worth first taking the time to consider what you really enjoy doing. Finding people with a similar outlook on life to yours is ⁶_____ easier if you do something you truly enjoy. Use your existing social network, but also look a ⁷_____ wider than that. Your friends can introduce you to other people who you might not have met otherwise.

B Complete the second sentence so it has the same meaning as the first. Use the word in parentheses.
1 If you exercise more, you'll be healthier. (THE)
_____ you'll be.
2 How old you are is important. How you feel is more important. (MUCH)
How you feel _____ .
3 Eating well is essential, and so is exercise. (JUST)
Eating well _____ .
4 Having good friends is much more beneficial than having many friends. (NOWHERE)
Having many friends _____ .
5 My brother and I used to be a bit closer than we are now. (QUITE)
My brother and I _____ .
6 Making friends face-to-face is a bit more difficult than making friends online. (SLIGHTLY)
Making friends online _____ .

C Match beginnings 1–6 to endings a–f.
1 What's the key to
2 I love seeing my friends, but while I'm studying, I try to limit myself to
3 After what Olivia said about Leon, he didn't want to
4 I'm really looking forward to
5 My grandma does a lot of charity work. She's really committed to
6 I would love to

a ☐ going out once a week.
b ☐ being happy when you retire?
c ☐ speak to her any more.
d ☐ live to be 100!
e ☐ helping others in her old age.
f ☐ retiring, I've had enough of work!

D Make it personal Complete the sentences so they're true for you.
1 The happier I am, _____ .
2 Having money is nowhere near as important as _____ .
3 I'm really looking forward to _____ .

10.3 How easy is it to make friends where you live?

A Read the text and check (✓) the reasons the writer gives for people not being very talkative.
1. ☐ They just like being quiet.
2. ☐ They lack social skills.
3. ☐ They prefer spending time with fewer people.
4. ☐ Relaxing makes them happy.
5. ☐ They're arrogant.

Why won't they talk to me?

It's a common misconception that being a quiet person is tantamount to being a shy person. The less you speak to others, the less confident you are. While it's true that shy people may be less talkative than most, it's ¹_____il logic al_____ to assume that all quiet people are shy. For some people, being quiet is just much more pleasant than talking a lot.

A frequently made assumption is that quiet people want to talk, but can't. A more sociable person might have an ²_____resist_____ urge to try to make them talk more by introducing them into a group conversation. But this often ends up being ³_____product_____, as it just puts them in the spotlight. They might beat around the bush, fumble their words, and sound awkward, which only serves to exacerbate the problem.

On the other hand, people often think that quiet people want to be left alone. But again, this is an ⁴_____rely_____ assumption. Just because someone doesn't talk much in a group doesn't mean he or she doesn't want to be around other people. Quiet people might just value quality over quantity when it comes to the number of friends they have. They prefer spending time with one or two close friends, and the feeling of ⁵_____depend_____ that that brings, rather than hanging out in large groups. If you have a quiet friend, you're lucky – it means he or she values you.

Another ⁶_____understand_____ that people have about quiet people is that they're unhappy or depressed. But think about the last time you had a really long, stressful day at work, or a party you've hosted where those last guests just seem to linger on. You just wanted to be alone and have some quiet time, right? Some people are just a little happier than others during down time.

So, if you know people who don't talk much, and you're worried about any of these things, get to know them on their terms. They might be shy and want help, but they might just be naturally quiet and perfectly happy. Either way, trying to force them out of their shell is ⁷_____accept_____ .

B Re-read and answer the questions. Is your experience with quiet people similar?

According to the writer ...
1. does encouraging quiet people to talk in groups make it easier or more difficult for them?
2. what's most important to quiet people when it comes to having friends?
3. in what situations do we all want to be alone?
4. what should we do if we're worried about quiet people?

C Complete highlighted words 1–7 in the text using a prefix from box A and a suffix from box B. Make any necessary spelling changes.

A

| counter ~~il~~ inter ir mis un (x2) |

B

| able (x2) ~~at~~ ence ible ing ive |

50

Have you ever met someone new by chance? 10.4

A 🔊40 Rewrite the underlined expressions using inversions and the word in parentheses. Listen to check.

Do you believe in fate?

Aaron

Absolutely. I've just had too many strange "coincidences" happen to me not to believe in fate. Like the time I got hit by a car, and then got up and walked away. ¹If I'd crossed the street (had) _____ a second sooner or later, I would have lost my life. Then there was the time I woke up late, despite being certain I'd set my alarm as usual. I rushed out the door, but it was too late. I'd missed my bus. ²If I had to have caught it (were) _____ , I wouldn't have ended up leaving my wallet in the taxi I ended up taking to work. Luckily, the next customer in the taxi found it and returned it to me at home. ³If she hadn't returned it (had) _____ , we wouldn't have met – and ended up getting married!

Fate? What a ridiculous notion! There's absolutely no evidence for it. People have coincidences, or bad luck that turns out well in the end, and they think there's some sort of destiny guiding them through life. Well, I'm sorry, but ⁴if we believed everything (were) _____ is planned out for us, then there would be no point in carrying on with life, if you ask me. I mean, what's the point in working hard, trying to make a difference, if our future is already mapped out for us? ⁵If you wish to believe (should) _____ in fate, do so by all means. But it's not for me.

Jaden

B Circle the correct options.

1 **A:** Thanks for all your help. It's been really useful.
  B: Not at all. Should you *have / had* any more questions, just give me a call.
2 **A:** Have you heard back from Lucy yet?
  B: No, it's been a week. *If she / Had she* enjoyed our date, she would have called me by now.
3 **A:** Are you and Hilary still not speaking?
  B: No, and I'm not planning on it, either. Were she *to apologize / apologized*, I might change my mind, though.
4 **A:** I can't believe I missed you at the party last night!
  B: I know! Were I to *stayed / have stayed* just five minutes longer, I would have seen you.
5 **A:** So you're saying you're actually pleased your car broke down?
  B: Yes! *Had I not / Hadn't I* taken the train to work instead, I wouldn't have met Fiona.

C Correct the mistake in these sentences. One sentence is correct.

1 At the start of every first date, the odds are not with you. _____
2 What are the odds that we would meet like this? _____
3 The odds of see her when I was in Mexico were like a million to 1! _____
4 The lottery's a waste of time. The odds are a billion of one you'll win. _____
5 What are the odds of turning up like this? _____

D Make it personal Complete the sentences so they're true for you.

1 Had I not come to class today, _____.
2 Were I to have met my best friend ten years ago, _____.
3 Had I stayed at home last weekend, _____.

10.5 How persuasive are you?

A Read and complete the persuasive essay with topic sentences 1–5. There's one extra sentence.

1 Where you position yourself when talking to someone is important, too.
2 As we all know, eye contact is important.
3 Communication is about so much more than words.
4 What you do with your hands says a lot about how you're feeling.
5 Copying what the other person does is another useful technique.

Using body language to get what you want

A ☐ Your body language expresses a lot about what you are thinking, and this happens whether you like it or not. A lot of research has been done that proves how we compose ourselves has an effect on what we can convey, and there are several ways we can use this to our advantage.

B ☐ Looking at someone directly can convey confidence and make people trust you. ¹*However / Moreover*, too much of this can intimidate the other person, and make him or her feel ill at ease. ²*However / Moreover*, it's not just about looking at someone. We can guide people to look at what we want them to look at by doing it ourselves. It's an old trick waiters use when they're showing you a menu – they look at the menu, not at you. Try it yourself some time.

C ☐ Standing too close to someone can make the person uncomfortable. ³*Finally / After all*, you don't want to infringe on his or her personal space. But standing directly in front of someone can have the same effect. People are more likely to want to continue speaking to you if you stand at an angle to them. ⁴*At this point / As we all know*, they'll feel comfortable in your company and want to listen to you.

D ☐ Also known as "mirroring." If you want to get people's attention, take a moment first to study their gestures. ⁵*Therefore / Next*, mimic what they do with their hands or how they're sitting. ⁶*Undoubtedly / As a result*, you don't want it to look like you're mocking them, and it's hard to get the balance just right. ⁷*Nevertheless / Next*, on a subconscious level, you'll make them feel like you're someone they can trust. ⁸*However / As a result*, they're more likely to take you seriously.

By now, you should have a range of techniques that you can use when in meetings, job interviews, and other important situations. Try some of them yourself in a more informal setting before putting them to the test in important ones.

B Re-read the essay and circle the correct options.

C Complete the sentences with these words.

as we all know	finally	however	next	therefore

1 Time is money. _____, you shouldn't make people wait longer than you have to.
2 _____, we're more likely to listen to people we trust.
3 First, greet people with a firm handshake. _____, offer them a seat. _____, you can get down to business.
4 Speak loudly enough for everyone to hear you. _____, don't shout!

D Look back at lessons 10.1–10.5 in the Student's Book. Find the connection between the song lines and the content of each lesson.

E ▶ 41 Listen to the five question titles from the unit, and record your answers to them. If possible, compare recordings with a classmate.

1 » 11.1 What was the last risk you took?

A ▶42 Listen to Aiden and Lily discussing the itinerary for an adventure trip in Costa Rica. Write the number of each day (1, 2, or 3) for each photo. There's one extra photo.

B ▶42 Listen again. True (T) or false (F)?
1 Lily doesn't think they should decide what to do on the first day until they arrive.
2 Aidan isn't going to go rafting.
3 During the rafting, they'll stop and walk through the jungle.
4 Lily thinks swimming with sharks is dangerous.
5 Aidan thinks the sharks might attack them.

C Correct the mistake in the extracts. Is each phrase used for hesitation (H) or encouragement (E)?
1 I'm not sure I get what it takes to jump straight into it like that. _____
2 I mean what's the worse that could happen? _____
3 These are man-eating fish. There's too much at stakes! _____
4 I mean, really, what have you gotten to lose? _____
5 I need to sleep in it before deciding. _____
6 Why not just go with a flow? _____

D Complete the conversations with one word in each blank.
1 **A:** What time does the film start?
   B: Eight, so we'd better leave at seven to be on the safe _____ .
2 **A:** Have you decided what you're going to do with your inheritance?
   B: Yes, I'm going to err on the side of _____ and keep it in my savings account for now.
3 **A:** Did you hear about Ben? He's doing a parachute jump!
   A: Really? He usually _____ it safe – doesn't sound like him at all.
4 **A:** Are you going to take the part in the play?
   B: Yes, but I'm keeping my day job, so I have a safety _____ to fall back on.
5 **A:** I want to do a bungee jump, but I'm worried it's not safe.
   B: Oh, don't worry. The people who run it are trained well. It's a safe _____ nothing bad will happen.

53

11.2 Do you enjoy riding a bike?

A Circle the correct option to complete the conversations.

1. **A:** You *might as well call / could have called* us. We were worried sick about you.
   B: I'm sorry, my phone died.
2. **A:** Where's Sally?
   B: I'm not sure. She *might / should* be here by now. She left an hour ago.
3. **A:** Oh, look at those dark clouds.
   B: I know. You *might / could* want to take your umbrella if you're going out.
4. **A:** What's the best way to get there?
   B: Take the bus. You *shouldn't / might* have to wait too long for one at that time.
5. **A:** Is there a lot of room in the back of the car?
   B: Yes, lots. We *might / should* as well take the bikes with us.
6. **A:** Which way should I go, do you think?
   B: Take the 105. There *could / shouldn't* be too much traffic at this time of day.

B Rephrase the underlined phrases in 1–6 using modals.

1. <u>I don't expect it will be difficult to get</u> there using public transportation.   *It shouldn't be difficult*
2. <u>We're annoyed that you didn't tell us</u> we didn't need to get here so early! _____
3. What can we do about Neil? <u>He refuses to get in</u> the car. _____
4. If there are four of us, <u>it would be a good idea to get</u> a taxi. It won't cost much. _____
5. <u>It's important to wear</u> a helmet when you're biking in the city. _____
6. <u>I expected Kate to have arrived</u> by now. _____

C Complete the text with the missing modals. There may be more than one answer.

If you're someone who generally ¹_____ leave the city on weekends, but, nevertheless, wants to get out and explore, you ²_____ want to try San Francisco Urban Trail Tours. We organize weekly mountain biking tours through the wonderful nature our city has to offer. San Francisco is one of the few cities where you experience the thrill of the trail without having to leave the city. With three levels – beginner, intermediate, and advanced, it ³_____ be difficult to enjoy yourself, whatever your level. You ⁴_____ want to bring your friends, too. So what are you waiting for? You ⁵_____ as well lace up and join us this weekend! Your only regret will be that you ⁶_____ have done this much earlier!

Urban trail tours

D Make it personal Complete the sentences so they're true for you.

1. It shouldn't be too difficult to _____.
2. My parents won't _____.
3. This weekend, I might as well _____.

54

Are you in favor of online dating? 11.3

A Read the article and match the headings to paragraphs 1–4. There's one extra heading.
a Being smart with your smart phone
b Training to make an impact
c Love (10,000 feet) in the air
d All aboard!
e Virtually yours

Innovative dating for today

Move over traditional dating. There are some new kids in town. It's estimated that more than 50% of Americans over 16 are single, and with more eligible adults than ever before, a number of novel new ways of finding your would-be partner are available. Here are what we think are some of the most interesting ones.

1 _____

This is similar to traditional speed-dating in that you have three minutes to speak to someone, screening a number of people throughout the evening. However, a "coach" is present, who feeds you a series of questions while you chat, so you don't need to strike up your own conversation and can avoid any awkward silences while you fumble for words. The questions themselves get increasingly personal (e.g. When was the last time you cried?), coaxing genuine and meaningful conversation from you that aims to go beyond just "small talk."

2 _____

Although traditional cruises have been around for a long time, singles cruises are specifically aimed at solo travelers who are looking for love or just to make new friends. They include games, speed-dating, and parties, and are generally popular with the 30–50 age range. The only problem with these is once you're on the ship, you're there for the duration. So if you don't like who you meet, you can't just leave. But at least you'll be on a cruise!

3 _____

The problem with online dating is the anonymity can attract unpleasant, menacing people, as well as genuine singles. You end up rolling the dice without much certainty a lot of the time. A new breed of apps, however, puts the woman in control. Once you match with someone, the woman has 24 hours to make contact or the connection is lost. If you change your mind, it's easy to bail. Another one asks users to answer a daily question. The woman can then choose whether to show her photo depending on the answers she reads.

4 _____

Though not yet a possibility, VR (Virtual Reality) dating is expected in the near future, as Internet speeds increase. This will allow you to go on a virtual reality date with someone, without having to leave the comfort of your abode. This will be a much safer way of getting to know each other before meeting for real.

B Circle the correct option to complete the sentences about the article.
1 *Over / Under* half of American adults are single.
2 Power dating, with a coach's support, requires you to be more *formal / intimate* than traditional speed dating.
3 It's *easy / difficult* to leave a singles cruise if you don't like it.
4 The new dating apps mean *more / fewer* strange people can make contact with you.
5 VR dating allows you to go on a date while you're at *home / a restaurant*.

C Match the highlighted words/phrases in the article to these meanings.
1 frightening, intimidating _____
2 start _____
3 available _____
4 evaluating to assess suitability _____
5 potential _____
6 home _____
7 escape _____
8 persuading _____
9 selecting something randomly _____

55

11.4 What does the sea make you think of?

A Complete the blanks with *a(n)*, *the*, or – (no article) and circle the correct options.

Five myths about "dangerous" animals you probably believe

ONE
¹_____ bees can attack you unprovoked.
²_____ general rule is that if you leave bees alone, they'll return the favor. The same isn't true for wasps, however. Depending on how close you are to their nest or the time of year, they might sting you for seemingly no reason.

TWO
Sharks are man-eaters.
³_____ shark attacks are very, very rare. In fact, ⁴_____ sad statistic is that for every human killed by sharks, around two million sharks are killed by ⁵_____ humans.

THREE
There are lots of dangerous ⁶*animal / animals* in Australia.
While ⁷_____ wildlife of Australia is rich and varied, only around three people die every year of wild animal related incidents, and most of ⁸*it / them* were caused by stupidity. In comparison, around 58 ⁹*of people / people* die in Australia every year from falling out of bed!

FOUR
Wolves are dangerous to people.
Wolves are generally afraid of people. In North America in the last 100 years, ¹⁰_____ record number of people have died from wolf attacks – two.

FIVE
Run in a zig-zag to escape from ¹¹_____ alligator.
Alligators generally avoid chasing people as they're too big to be appropriate food. But if one does chase you, run in a straight line and very fast – in ¹²_____ opposite direction, of course!

B Correct the mistake in these sentences. Two sentences are correct.
1 I had terrible flight a few years ago, and now I'm afraid of flying.
2 I worry about diseases a lot now that I'm getting older.
3 I've had a lot of advice about how to stay safe when traveling, but most of them wasn't very useful.
4 There has been record number of burglaries in my area recently, and that really worries me.
5 I know it sounds silly, but I'm afraid of the dark!

C ▶43 Complete the conversations with one word in each blank. Listen to check.
1 **A:** I'm reading _____ interesting article about fear and the human brain at the moment.
   B: Is that _____ article that was in *Scientist* magazine? I think I saw that.
2 **A:** Why do you think _____ rich tend to live longer?
   B: Better access to healthcare, I'd say. Most of _____ have good medical plans.
3 **A:** Are you enjoying your new job as _____ engineer?
   B: It's interesting work, though some of _____ can be quite dangerous.
4 **A:** We can take a short cut through _____ forest.
   B: No, it's too dark. That's not _____ risk I want to take.

D Make it personal Complete the sentences so they're true for you.
1 I'm sometimes afraid of _____.
2 The rich in my country should do more to _____.

56

Have you ever had an allergic reaction? 11.5

A Read the statistical report and answer the questions.

1 At what age are adults particularly at risk of accidents? _____
2 Where do falls usually occur? _____
3 For how long is a hot drink potentially dangerous to children? _____
4 What else can cause burns to children? _____
5 In which part of the house do the fewest accidents occur? _____

▲ ▲ ▲ ▲ ▲ ▲ ▲ ACCIDENTS IN THE HOME ▲ ▲ ▲ ▲ ▲ ▲ ▲

The number of injuries that ¹*occur / occurs* at home is higher than for any other location. Every year, approximately 20,000 people die because of accidents at home. More than four million children under the age of 15 experience accidents in and around the home every year and need to be taken to emergency rooms. One out of every five homes ²*report / reports* an accident each month.

Children under 5 and adults over 65 (most of these ³*is / are* over 75) are those who are most at risk. Most of the accidents with children ⁴*involve / involves* boys, while most of the accidents with adults ⁵*happen / happens* to women.

By room, the number of accidents in the home break down as follows:

LOCATIONS OF ACCIDENTS IN THE HOME	
Room/Area	Percent
Lounge	25
Kitchen	15
Bedroom	5
Bathroom	10
Stairs	35

The most common accidents involve falls. Half of these ⁶*is / are* on the stairs and the other half ⁷*is / are* from windows. Falls can be very serious and require medical attention. Unfortunately, some of the adults who fall ⁸*live / lives* alone, and may not be able to call for help immediately, especially if they lose consciousness.

A number of accidents with children ⁹*is / are* from burns or scalds, and some of these ¹⁰*include / includes* burns from hot drinks. A hot drink can scald a child for up to 15 minutes afterwards. Some of the burns also come from faulty electrical equipment, especially heaters.

There are a number of steps you can take to improve safety in and around the home, for example:

- Don't put heavy objects in high places.
- Keep windows closed when children are unattended.
- Use stair "gates" with small children.
- Use a cordless kettle so children can't pull the cord.
- Have all heaters checked for safety once a year.

For more advice and information, visit **www.saferhomes.id**

B Re-read the report and circle the correct options.

C Complete the conversations with these words. There's one extra.

> cramps   doom   hives   swelling   wheezing

1 **A:** What's that rash on your arm?
   B: It's _____. I often get them when it's cold like this.
2 **A:** Keep applying this cream, and the _____ should go down in a day or two.
   B: Thanks, doctor.
3 **A:** I've got an impending sense of _____ about the exam.
   B: Me too, I don't think I've studied enough.
4 **A:** Are you OK?
   B: Not really, I've got stomach _____. I think that fish I ate was bad.

D Look back at lessons 11.1–11.5 in the Student's Book. Find the connection between the song lines and the content of each lesson.

E ⓘ 44 Listen to the five question titles from the unit, and record your answers to them. If possible, compare recordings with a classmate.

12 » 12.1   What brands are the wave of the future?

A ▶45 Listen to a webinar on successful brand building. Number steps a–f in the order they are discussed. There's one extra step.

a ☐ Stand out from the crowd.
b ☐ Stay true to your brand.
c ☐ Reward your customers.
d ☐ Create your mission statement.
e ☐ Do your market research.
f ☐ Create a logo.

B ▶45 Listen again and choose the correct answer (a, b, or c).

1 Brands that do well sell to …
  a particular sectors of society.
  b as broad a market as possible.
  c both adults and children.
2 Building a brand your customers can identify with is important …
  a for short-term success.
  b for long-term success.
  c for both short and long-term success.
3 A mission statement is _____ a logo.
  a the same as
  b shorter than
  c different from
4 You need to study the competition so that you can …
  a sell more cheaply than other companies.
  b provide what's lacking.
  c copy their best practices.
5 A logo should …
  a help people identify you easily.
  b be simple.
  c be funny.
6 Your long-term practices should …
  a change regularly.
  b reflect your mission statement.
  c try to appeal to everyone.

C Complete the extracts from the podcast with one word in each blank.

1 All successful brand building _____ from detailed studies on the characteristics and typical behavior of the target market.
2 If you get this right, it will not only get you noticed at the beginning, but will also _____ the way for future brand loyalty.
3 While this statement might be _____ related to your slogan, it's not the same thing.
4 Maintaining your core values in practice will give _____ to strong brand loyalty, which is vital for long-term success.

D Look at the table. Then circle the correct options in 1–5.

Year	Sales of 3D TVs (millions)
2012	0.5
2013	15
2014	25
2015	12.9
2016	9.7
2017	9.6

1 After a bumpy start, sales of 3D TVs *skyrocketed / plummeted* in 2013.
2 In 2014, they continued to *level off / soar* to 25 million.
3 In 2015, sales *rose / plunged* to 12.9 million.
4 They continued to *fall / soar* in 2016 to 9.7 million.
5 Since then, they have *leveled off / risen* to about this same number..

What songs have changed the world? 12.2

A Complete 1–5 with the verbs in parentheses. Use passive forms with a gerund or an infinitive. Any surprises?

Sometimes songs don't mean what you think they do

It's often easy to interpret song lyrics how we want to, and some would argue that's the real beauty of music – that it can mean different things to different people. But sometimes we get it totally wrong.

Take U2's critically acclaimed One. ¹_____ (interpret) as a love song leads to it often being played at weddings. It would seem lead singer Bono objects to it ² _____ (use) this way, however. When he heard from fans about it, he replied, "Are you mad? It's about splitting up!"

While not a misinterpretation as such, 2012 K-Pop classic Gangnam Style has a deeper meaning than most expect. With its catchy dance track and signature move, it's easy ³ _____ (see) as a lighthearted, funny song. However, it should ⁴ _____ (not consider) this way, as it's actually a satire on South Korean society and those who enjoy ⁵ _____ (see) as wealthy, despite not having much money and having fallen into debt.

B Use the prompts to complete the sentences.

1 We just released our new single, and we're [look forward / to / it / play] _____ on the radio.
2 We expected our first album [play] _____ everywhere, but it didn't do very well in the end.
3 [offer] _____ a recording contract was the highlight of our career.
4 The song's explicit lyrics meant it [could / not / play] _____ on the radio.
5 After our "joke" song Hilda's Eggs, we found it [difficult / take] _____ seriously as a band again.
6 This song is about the fact that we [couldn't stand / reject] _____ so often by record producers.

C Complete the crossword with the missing phrasal verbs in the clues. Refer to Student's Book page 128.

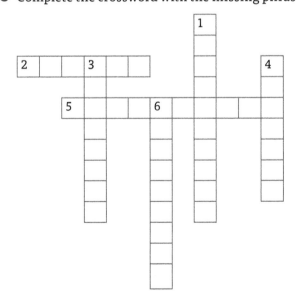

ACROSS
2 I didn't enjoy the book at first, but it slowly began to _____ _____ me.
5 It was an important song which helped raise awareness and _____ _____ real change for the better.

DOWN
1 As some artists get older, they _____ _____ _____ their earlier success rather than trying something completely new.
3 The audience wasn't very enthusiastic at first, but after the second song, they started to _____ _____ _____ the band.
4 It wasn't until their third album that the band's music began to _____ _____ .
6 The message that the story tries to _____ _____ is one of hope in difficult circumstances.

D Make it personal Complete the sentences so they're true for you.

1 I would enjoy being thought of as _____ .
2 When I die, I hope to be remembered for _____ .
3 I really object to _____ .

12.3 What futuristic programs have you seen?

A Read the article and check (✓) the statement which best reflects the writer's opinion.
1. ☐ Change is good, but not if it happens too quickly.
2. ☐ We should avoid change unless it's only for the greater good.
3. ☐ There are both positive and negative effects of change.

The future's bright – or is it?

1. It's an undisputed fact that the world is changing and will continue to do so at an unprecedented rate. Every day we make giant leaps in key areas, namely science, technology, and medicine. For the most part these changes are positive, exciting, and aimed at the greater good. But more prescient futurologists are drawing attention to the downsides, too.

2. Take driverless cars, for example. Once considered to be a wacky idea, they're now already becoming a reality. They're generally thought to be much safer as they eliminate the pitfalls of human error caused by distraction and fatigue. Cars will be able to make calculated decisions on speed instead of responding to random human reactions. But they also raise important moral questions. Let's say your driverless car is forced to swerve from a hazard in order to save you. Would it still do so if it meant hitting a pedestrian? Will its primary function be to save the driver or the public?

3. Another growing trend is that of fitness trackers, which monitor your exercise and sleep patterns. A recent case in the U.S. showed that the data collected can be used as evidence in court. A woman called 911 and claimed an intruder broke into her house while she was asleep, when, in fact, the tracker showed she was up and walking about normally. There are even apps that work with trackers specifically aimed at providing you with an alibi. But what kind of people want to provide alibis? Also, what's to stop someone from framing you for a crime by stealing your tracker?

4. Virtual Reality (VR) is another technology which is undergoing serious development at the moment. It has lots of useful applications such as gaming, training surgeons, and even dating. However, many farsighted people argue that there needs to be a lot more research done into the effects on the human brain. We already know that it gets your eyes to work in different ways from what is normal and alters your perception of distance. It's therefore dangerous to drive immediately after using a VR headset.

5. We should definitely encourage change and development, but it's worth remembering that with great change comes great opportunity, but only if it's managed appropriately and studied properly.

B Re-read the article. True (T) or false (F)?
1. The rate of change is getting slower.
2. People once thought driverless cars weren't a serious idea.
3. The example given shows that driverless cars are more dangerous for everyone.
4. The woman who called 911 was sleeping when the crime occurred.
5. The writer suggests that fitness trackers could be used in crimes.
6. The writer thinks VR headsets provide harmless entertainment.

C Find words in the article to match these definitions.
1. advances, developments made quickly (par.1) _____ (n)
2. specifically (par.1) _____ (adv)
3. having knowledge of events before they take place (par.1) _____ (adj)
4. silly, crazy (par.2) _____ (adj)
5. hidden or unseen dangers (par.2) _____ (n)
6. done without planning (par.2) _____ (adj)
7. experiencing (par.4) _____ (v)
8. having awareness of future possibilities (par.4) _____ (adj)

How unpredictable has your life been? 12.4

A ▶46 Complete the conversation using the prompts in parentheses. Listen to check.

PENNY: Hey Mike, I heard you ¹_____ (get / promote) to store manager recently.
MIKE: Yes! It was a real surprise, I can tell you.
PENNY: Oh yeah? Why's that?
MIKE: Honestly, a few weeks ago I thought I was going to ²_____ (get / fire)! I ³_____ (have / some work / do) on my apartment at the time and having to sleep on the sofa. I kept waking up late and then showing up late for work. My boss wasn't happy and I kept ⁴_____ (get / hassle) about it. And I ⁵_____ (have / my work / criticize), too, by him, because he was in a bad mood, which made me feel really pressured.
PENNY: Oh, I never realized. So what changed?
MIKE: Well, one night the store ⁶_____ (be / break into). We were looking through the CCTV and I recognized the people on the video. So I ⁷_____ (get / the police / involve) and told them everything I knew about them.
PENNY: Really? And they were arrested?
MIKE: Exactly. And my boss ⁸_____ (have / all the stolen items / recover). Anyway, needless to say, I was back in good standing, and when the manager's position became available, he gave it to me!
PENNY: Congratulations!

B Correct the mistake in these sentences. One sentence is correct.
1 Be careful crossing the road. You could have hurt if you don't look both ways. _____
2 If you don't keep up repayments, you could have repossessed your house. _____
3 I just had my manuscript accepted by the publisher! I'd almost given up hope. _____
4 After catching the thieves, Gary had his photo took with the store owner. _____
5 Don't do that here. Do you want to get arrested us? _____
6 Joanna was been pressured constantly by her boss before she suddenly announced she was leaving. _____

C Match 1–5 to endings a–e to form sentences.
1 I'm not going to drive all the way there for a 30-minute meeting. It's just not
2 Studying coding at school is really
3 I didn't think it would be worth
4 Is it worth my
5 Is it worth the

a ☐ entering the competition, but I ended up winning first prize!
b ☐ effort of calling the police? I don't think there's anything they can do.
c ☐ worth it.
d ☐ time watching this movie? I've heard it's good, but it's three hours long!
e ☐ worthwhile for kids today, given the uncertain job market in the future.

D Make it personal Complete the sentences so they're true for you.
1 The last time I had my photo taken _____.
2 I hate being pressured to _____.
3 I try to avoid getting hurt by _____.

61

12.5 What will make a better society?

A Rewrite a–e using a noun phrase.

a the number of people who work outside the home has declined steadily
there has been a steady decline in the number of people who work outside the home

b the number of people using social media has increased hugely
_____

c criticisms of its effect on our well being have risen steadily
_____

d the number of "clickbait" articles has increased dramatically
_____

e the number of work opportunities has risen steeply
_____

B Read and complete the opinion essay with your sentences from A.

Does social media make us happier?

1 Love it or loathe it: ¹☐ in recent times. With the increased use ²☐. Does it make us happier or sadder? Many say we now have shorter attention spans; we're more likely to be jealous of others; and we end up making unreasonable comparisons between ourselves and those we see online. I would argue, however, that the benefits far outweigh these criticisms.

2 In recent years ³☐, especially in office jobs. Many people are choosing to work from home. Access to social media makes people feel less isolated and allows them to stay connected with the outside world. It's also a way of making new connections. As someone who works from home myself, I have noticed ⁴☐, which came about through connections made on social media. This is work I wouldn't have gotten in a 9–5 office job.

3 I also believe that it has forced us to become better at critical thinking – ⁵☐. These articles use sensationalist titles and often contain spurious, unchecked facts. This might seem like a bad thing at first, but as more and more hoaxes and false news stories are exposed, people become more aware and more likely to fact-check them before sharing.

4 In conclusion, whether it really makes us happier or not, it's incredibly popular and unlikely to go away any time soon. While many fears about social media are real, I genuinely believe that overall it's a positive force.

C Re-read the opinion essay and answer the questions. Do you agree with the author?

1 What three negative effects of social media are given in the introduction (paragraph 1)?
_____

2 What two benefits of social media are given in paragraph 2?
_____

3 What negative aspects of "clickbait" articles are described?
_____

D Look back at lessons 12.1–12.5 in the Student's Book. Find the connection between the song lines and the content of each lesson.

E ▶47 Listen to the five question titles from the unit, and record your answers to them. If possible, compare recordings with a classmate.

Selected audio scripts

▶ **27** *page 33 exercises A and B*

P = Presenter, S = Scott, A = Adriana,
D = Darrell, M = Martha

P: Good morning, and welcome to the *Voices* podcast, where we discuss the issues that affect you. In the last episode, we talked about milestones in life, and how we view the importance of different stages of life differently. Well, we decided to go out into the neighborhood and ask people what their most important milestones have been.

P: Scott

S: Oh, no doubt about it. For me it was having little Lucy, my pride and joy. Until then I'd been kind of just sailing through life, you know? I just took one job after another, not really having any hopes or ambitions. But when Lucy was born, all of a sudden the stakes were higher. Now I had to put someone else before me in every way. So I worked hard, put myself through college in the evenings and got a much better job.

P: Adriana

A: I've always worked really hard, so when I lost my job a few years' back it was a huge shock. I had a lot of time to sit and reflect, and see how far I'd gotten off track. It took me a long time to come to terms with the situation, especially when I kept getting rejected each time I applied for something new, which made it even harder. But I'm pleased to say that I'm now working again though, and I love my job!

P: Darrell

D: Last year, after forty years of service as a bank manager, I finally decided to call it a day. At first it was really hard, because all of a sudden you've got this big, work-shaped hole in your life, you know? But that didn't last long. Fortunately, I've never been one to wallow in self-pity, and I decided I had to take charge of my situation, really take the bull by the horns, you know? I started joining clubs here and there, taking up new interests, just doing all the things I'd always wanted to. Phew! Well, I don't think I've ever been busier – nor happier!

P: Martha

M: The most important thing I've ever done, without a shadow of a doubt, was living in Brazil for two years, teaching English. Boy was it a culture shock! Until that time, I'd never even left my hometown, not even once! Being in that new situation as a foreigner, it was like being a fish out of water. I had to learn a new language, assimilate into a new culture, everything. And I won't lie to you. At times it was really tough. But I made it through the hard times. In the end I really felt like I came of age during that time. It made me a more mature person, as a result, and I'm better able to appreciate other people's differences.

▶ **31** *page 38 exercises A and B*

P = Presenter, C = Cameron

P: In the studio with me today is Cameron Mathis, from the Movement Against Patronizing Advertisements, or MAPA. So, Cameron, am I right in thinking you don't like advertising in general?

C: Oh no, in fact that's a common misconception about our organization. We do understand the need for advertising in a competitive market. In fact, some of the commercials you see currently taking the Internet by storm are really rather good. On top of that, there are a multitude of services many of us use today that are free, thanks to the revenue generated by advertising.

P: So, what is it you're taking a stand against then?

C: Well, what we really take offense at is the way commercials seem to want to treat us like children.

P: How do you mean, exactly?

C: Take company mascots, for example. You've got an airline that uses a cartoon-style plane with a big, sappy face on the front, grinning inanely at us like it's right out of a children's book. I mean, aren't we intelligent enough to understand what an airplane is? Then you have the workers in a commercial for an electric company with juvenile, smiling faces and huge eyes. These images wouldn't look out of place in a children's TV show, but in commercials? To make matters worse, they speak in clichés, use childish language and speak directly to us like we're infants. And to add insult to injury, they all come together at the end to sing a catchy jingle that sounds more like a nursery rhyme.

P: But what's the problem, really? Surely they're just aiming for a broad appeal?

C: The problem, aside from the lack of respect for their consumers, is it's leading to a general dumbing-down of society. When people are bombarded with these images and sounds all day, every day, they begin to feel they're acceptable. And as if that wasn't enough, people accept some of the ridiculous claims made by these companies. You know the sort of thing I mean, "This sugary drink will make you healthier." The people behind these ads really need to take the blame for this.

P: But aren't some ads specifically aimed at children?

C: Some are, yes. But how many children do you know with a mortgage or with bills to pay?

P: I get your point. So, what does MAPA intend to do? Take legal action against companies that advertise in this way?

C: Oh, no, no, no. For a start, we're not out to make money off this. Besides, it's not a legal issue. It's a moral and cultural one. And since people create culture, it's people who need to take matters into their own hands. Don't buy products from companies that treat you like a child. Write to them or post on their social media, asking them why they view us like this. We need to take a stand against this together, and that's why we're trying to raise awareness with our own campaigns. We're not idiots, after all. And it's time they stopped treating us as if we were.

P: Cameron, thanks very much for joining us today.

C: Thank you.

▶ **34** *page 43 exercises B and C*

J = Jasmin (newsreader), H = Henry (reporter), D = Dorothy (school principal)

J: In education news, the government has announced plans to introduce regular mindfulness training in elementary schools as part of the state curriculum. It says that recent studies have shown that regular mindfulness training in schools helps children become calm, focused, and creative so that they work better both in class and at home. Over to our education correspondent, Henry Coleman, with more information on the story.

H: Thanks, Jasmin. I'm here at Grangeville Elementary, where in the last year students have been having regular mindfulness classes as part of their daily routine. And joining me is the school principal, Dorothy Quinn, to tell us more about it. Good morning, Dorothy. How did this project come about?

D: Good morning. Well, we decided to introduce the training a year ago. There was some opposition from a few parents at the time, who felt it was a waste of time in the school day, so we decided to make it optional, and about half the children took part. We felt the benefits would outweigh the time factor, and, so far at least, it would appear that we've been proved right.

H: Interesting. So, what happens in a mindfulness class?

D: We usually start with what we call "deep-belly breathing". The children put their hands on their stomachs and we ask them to focus on their breathing, feeling the air being drawn in. They then look at their hands, and we ask them to admire their form and what they do. Then we move on to simple stretching and walk slowly around the room, while they continue to focus on their breathing.

H: It looks as if it's quite simple.

D: It does, but believe me, it takes a lot of concentration.

H: So, what benefits have you found from the training?

D: Well, for starters, the children in the program consistently outperform those who opted out, both on tests and in day-to-day schoolwork.

H: Really?

D: Yes. In fact, as the program continued and parents started seeing a difference, more and more children joined the program, and they now outnumber considerably those who didn't take part. We're also finding that their concentration levels outlast the others, too. They're able to focus for much longer

65

Selected audio scripts

in class. We've also been using the training to replace some traditional discipline punishments, too.
H: In what way?
D: Well, if a child was particularly unruly in class before, or got in trouble for something, he or she might have had detention for an hour after school, doing extra work. We've replaced that with a mindfulness session, and have found that these kids outgrow their immature behavior much more quickly. Rather than trying to outsmart the teachers and break the rules, they're being much more cooperative.
H: This all sounds fascinating, Dorothy, thank you. I may try it myself!
D: You should!

▶ 38 page 48 exercises A and B

R = Ron, E = Eva

R: Did I ever tell you about my so-called friend James, the one I had at high school?
E: No, you didn't. Why "so-called"?
R: Well, I guess it goes without saying he was the worst friend I've ever had.
E: Why? What did he do?
R: Well, I met him during my senior year. He had just moved to the area and just started at our school. He was a breath of fresh air, really livened up the place.
E: Why do you say that?
R: Er, he was just really good fun. The life of the party, you know? We hit it off immediately. We went out at weekends and he took me to parties. Oh, what a riot he was!
E: So, why wasn't he a good friend?
R: After a while, the cracks in our friendship started to appear. Like, he kept insisting on coming over to my house rather than going out or to his. And he started being really critical of everything I did. Sometimes he'd just try to embarrass me, you know? It goes without saying that I was starting to get a bit suspicious. Anyway, one day he was over and we were playing a video game. All of a sudden he just got up and left, no words, nothing. Later that evening I realized my camera had disappeared.
E: Oh no, had he taken it?
R: I think so, though I can never be sure. I looked everywhere, and I remember I'd showed it to him the day before.
E: So, did you confront him about it?
R: Easier said than done! He stopped talking to me at school and was always surrounded by another group of friends. I know I should have said something, but, truth be told, I just felt too embarrassed, you know, and betrayed.
E: Oh, that's awful. You know I lost a good friend too, once.
R: Really? What happened?

▶ 39 page 48 exercise C

R: Really? What happened?
E: It was my best friend, Judy. We went back a long way. I mean we'd been friends since we were five. We went everywhere together, you know? Real birds of a feather.
R: Yeah, I've had a couple of friends like that.
E: Yeah, and we really understood each other, you know? Our conversations always went beneath the surface. I mean we didn't always see eye to eye, but we understood each other – sometimes without even having to speak.
R: So, what happened?
E: When we were in our early twenties, she met this guy –
R: Ah-ha!
E: No, I mean we'd both had boyfriends before, but always stayed close. But this time it was different. She would spend all her time with him. It got to the point where she stopped returning my calls. I was really upset and I really missed her.
R: Are they still together?
E: I have no idea. Last I heard he had gotten a new job in Illinois, and they moved there. I haven't heard from her since.
R: Oh, that's sad.
E: Yeah, it is. But at least we have each other now, right?
R: That goes without saying!

▶ 42 page 53 exercises A and B

A = Aiden, L = Lily

A: So, what's first on the itinerary then?
L: OK, well, we arrive in the capital, San José, at lunchtime, and then spend the day there relaxing. We can either go sightseeing or just explore the area near the hotel. Best to just see how we feel when we get there, I think. Then the next morning, first thing, we head out to the Pacuare River for white-water rafting.
A: Wow, OK …
L: What's wrong?
A: Um … it's just that I've never done it before, and the brochure says it's a tough river, not for beginners. I'm not sure I have what it takes to jump straight into it like that.
L: Really? We could just play it safe and go on one of the calmer rivers if you like.
A: Ah no, it's fine. Let's throw caution to the wind. It's supposed to be an adventure vacation after all, right? I mean, what's the worst that could happen?
L: That's the spirit! And it's all organized by a reputable company with trained first-aid personnel in case anything goes wrong … so there's kind of a safety net. Also, the river goes through the jungle, and you can see all sorts of animals like toucans and howler monkeys.
A: Fantastic. So, what's next?
L: OK, so Day 3 we go to Cahuita National park, and go hiking through the jungle for a few hours in the morning and end up at the beach. In the afternoon, we need to decide what we're going to do. There's snorkeling, zip lining and even swimming with sharks!
A: Ooh, I like the sound of that.
L: Really? I think it sounds terrifying! These are man-eating fish. There's too much at stake!
A: Don't be silly, they wouldn't let you swim with them if it was dangerous in any way. It's a safe bet they won't attack you. I mean really, what have you got to lose?
L: Hmmm, not sure. I need to sleep on it before deciding.
A: Well, we don't have to decide until we're there, do we? Why not just go with the flow? We can see what other people are doing.
L: OK then, good idea. So, day 4 …

▶ 45 page 58 exercises A and B

Hello, and welcome to the latest webinar in the *Building your Business* series. Today we're going to be looking at building a successful brand in five simple steps. This is one of the most important aspects of your new business. If you get it right, you'll see sales of your product soar. So, if you're ready, let's begin. If you have any questions, please type them in the chat box and I'll answer them at the end of the webinar.

Step 1 – All successful brand building stems from detailed studies on the characteristics and typical behavior of the target market. Almost all successful brands are aimed at specific, niche markets. Find out what your potential customers' values and desires are, and then create a brand image they can relate to. If you get this right, it will not only get you noticed at the beginning, but will also pave the way for future brand loyalty. We'll come back to this later.

Step 2 – Figure out exactly what your core values are and how to express them concisely in a mission statement. This is an important foundation for all your future work, so don't rush it. While this statement might be closely related to your slogan, it's not the same thing. For example, Nike's slogan is "Just Do It", whereas its mission statement is, "to bring inspiration and innovation to every athlete in the world."

Step 3 – Differentiate your product from other brands. You need a USP – a unique selling point – and again this means doing your research, this time on the competition. Find out what your closest competitors do well, and what they don't do so well, as this is where you can come in and fill the gap. If your brand is too similar to others in the market, you may well find that after any initial success, the novelty will wear off and sales will plummet.

Step 4 – While it may seem obvious, the next step is perhaps the most important part of brand building. It's worth spending considerable time and money on it. You want something which clearly embodies the values and mission of your business. You also want something which is attractive and easily recognizable.

Step 5 – If you've followed all the steps so far, then you've built the foundations for a successful brand. But that's only the beginning. An outsider should be able to read your mission statement, look at what you do and see a perfect match. Maintaining your core values in practice will give rise to strong brand loyalty, which is vital for long-term success. A big product launch can cause sales to skyrocket, but long-term brand loyalty is important for continued success, even if it just means that sales level off to profitable numbers. Be true to your customers, and they'll be loyal to you.

OK, so I see we have some questions coming in. Let's start with this one from …

Answer key

Unit 7

7.1
A 1 b 2 a 3 b 4 c
B 1 Adriana 2 Darrell 3 Martha
  4 Adriana 5 Scott 6 Martha
C 1 came of age 2 take charge of
  3 gotten off track 4 the stakes were higher
  5 come to terms with 6 made it through
D 1 rat 2 worms 3 cat 4 chickened
  5 horse's
E Students' own answers

7.2
A 1 will have gotten 2 will have been acknowledged 3 will have had
  4 will have exercised / been exercising
  5 won't have been 6 will have lived
B 1 will have been earned 2 will have been traveling traveled 3 Correct 4 won't have been coming come 5 will have worked / will have been working 6 will have been allocated
C 1 will have been working 2 will have retired 3 will have been fired, will have been forced 4 will have saved 5 will have lost
D Students' own answers

7.3
A dishonest
B 1 C 2 D 3 B 4 extra sentence 5 E
  6 A
C 1 facial 2 informed 3 daily
  4 evolutionary 5 crucial 6 early
  7 rudimentary 8 unfair 9 fair

7.4
A 1 It's not how old you are that
  2 It wasn't the first time that
  3 It's not just young people who
  4 It was 100-year-old Ida Keeling who
  5 It's not your age that
  6 It's only your belief in yourself
B 1 only respect that I feel
  2 your attitude that determines
  3 their perspective on life that
  4 a belief in themselves that
  5 their achievements that leave
C 1 act 2 pushing 3 conform 4 hand
  5 wise 6 heart
D Students' own answers

7.5
A experience
B 1 response 2 suited 3 see 4 fit
  5 capacity 6 consideration
C 1 receptive 2 proactive 3 attentive
  4 dynamic
D 1 possibly 2 interrupting 3 kind
  4 run 5 Would
E 1 getting married (life stages)
  2 the future and the grammar: converting future continuous to future perfect continuous 3 babies 4 human behavior
  5 jobs and making a living
F Students' own answers

Unit 8

8.1
A 1, 3, 5, 6
B 1 F 2 T 3 T 4 F 5 F 6 T
C 1 c 2 a, b 3 a 4 e 5 d
D 1 matters 2 top 3 enough 4 insult
E Students' own answers

8.2
A 1 make 2 that 3 refund 4 weren't
  5 look
B 1 you listen to your customers 2 your company give me a refund 3 you make customers aware of your policy first 4 this dress weren't so expensive 5 you be more polite when taking orders 6 you give me a bigger seat
C 1 know 2 reassess 3 write 4 wasn't
  5 be 6 give
D Students' own answers

8.3
A 1 e 2 b 3 c 4 a
B 1 worse 2 meal time 3 the flight attendant asks them not to 4 used baby products 5 acceptable
C 1 lengths 2 upon 3 saw 4 way
  5 take

8.4
A 1 For all the 2 Whatever 3 However
  4 As useful as 5 Much as
B 1 d 2 b 3 e 4 a 5 c
C Across: 1 profit 3 charge 5 borrow
  6 tax
  Down: 2 inherit 4 loan

8.5
A 3
B 1 rectify 2 avail 3 fact 4 resolve
  5 happy 6 satisfaction 7 legal 8 steps
  9 forward
C 1 avail 2 assist 3 a response
  4 Notwithstanding 5 resolve / rectify
D 1 bad customer service and advertising
  2 the grammar: *wish* + subjunctive
  3 travel and being far away
  4 making ends meet / money and the grammar: combining sentences with adverb clauses
  5 getting satisfaction by phone
E Students' own answers

Unit 9

9.1
A 1
B 1 d 2 b 3 a 4 c
C 1 b 2 c 3 a 4 a 5 b
D 1 outweigh 2 outperform 3 outnumber
  4 outlast 5 outgrow 6 outsmart
E Students' own answers

9.2
A 1 are believed to help you
  2 can be expected to make you
  3 is known to be effective
  4 are thought to be good
  5 is believed to hydrate your body
  6 is known to come from other sources
  7 was reported to make kids
B 1 are reported to be successful
  2 are thought to use
  3 is believed to be
  4 is known not to work.
C 1 coming down with 2 grew out of
  3 watching out for 4 go through with
  5 gave up on
D Students' own answers

9.3
A 2
B 1 Darren 2 Mike 3 Angela 4 Celia
C 1 F 2 F 3 T 4 F 5 T
D 1 ending 2 desire 3 belief
  4 discussion 5 choices 6 blanket
  7 mate 8 rearing

9.4
A 1 to change 2 from doing 3 make
  4 to replace 5 on keeping 6 to start
  7 not to do 8 do 9 his 10 enjoy
B 1 dissuaded me **from** eating 2 stopping to stop 3 you to join 4 to eat from eating
  5 Correct 6 lift lifting
C 1 threaten 2 weaken 3 worsen
  4 soften 5 lengthen 6 strengthen
  7 freshen
D Students' own answers

9.5
A against
B 1 Weight loss 2 Confidence
  3 Awareness 4 Education 5 provide
  6 lead 7 create 8 slow
C 1 weight loss lose weight
  2 Provide a A safe environment:
  3 concentration concentrate at work better.
D 1 correctly 2 mind 3 judgment
E 1 *out-* verbs 2 three word phrasal verbs (*give up on*) 3 surviving challenging situations 4 the grammar: overview of verb patterns (pattern a) 5 celebrating beauty regardless of weight, etc.
F Students' own answers

Unit 10

10.1
A 1 Ron's camera 2 He stopped talking to Ron.
B 1 Ron 2 James 3 James 4 James
  5 James 6 Ron
C 1 They'd been friends since they were five.
  2 Sometimes they understood each other without the need to speak.
  3 Judy met her boyfriend in their early twenties.
  4 Judy stopped returning her calls.
  5 Judy and her boyfriend moved to Illinois.

69

Answer key

D 1 c 2 a 3 f 4 e 5 g 6 b 7 d
E 1 telling 2 said 3 told 4 saying
   5 Say

10.2
A 1 the harder 2 whole 3 near
   4 every bit 5 quite 6 far 7 bit
B 1 The more you exercise, the healthier you'll be.
   2 How you feel is much more important than how old you are.
   3 Eating well is just as essential as exercising / exercise (verb or noun).
   4 Having many friends is nowhere near as beneficial as having good friends.
   5 My brother and I aren't quite as close as we used to be.
   6 Making friends online is slightly easier than making friends face-to-face.
C 1 b 2 a 3 c 4 f 5 e 6 d
D Students' own answers

10.3
A Check 1, 3 and 4.
B 1 more difficult
   2 quality (over quantity)
   3 after a long day at work or a party that goes on too long
   4 get to know them on their own terms
C 1 illogical 2 irresistible
   3 counterproductive 4 unreliable
   5 interdependence 6 misunderstanding
   7 unacceptable

10.4
A 1 Had I crossed the street
   2 Were I to have caught it
   3 Had she not returned it
   4 Were we to believe everything
   5 Should you wish to believe
B 1 have 2 Had she 3 to apologize
   4 have stayed 5 Had I not
C 1 ~~not with~~ against 2 correct 3 ~~see~~ seeing 4 billion ~~of~~ to one 5 the odds of **[subject]** turning up
D Students' own answers

10.5
A A 3 B 2 C 1 D 5
B 1 However 2 Moreover 3 After all
   4 At this point 5 Next 6 Undoubtedly
   7 Nevertheless 8 As a result
C 1 Therefore 2 As we all know
   3 Next, Finally 4 However
D 1 the nature of friendship 2 the life span (living forever) 3 double affixation (un- and -ful) 4 the grammar: inverted conditional sentences 5 persuading someone
E Students' own answers

Unit 11
11.1
A 1 d 2 a 3 c
B 1 T 2 F 3 F 4 T 5 F
C 1 ~~get~~ have, H 2 ~~worse~~ worst, E 3 ~~stakes~~ stake, H 4 ~~gotten~~ got, E 5 ~~in~~ on, H
   6 ~~a~~ the, E

D 1 side 2 caution 3 plays 4 net 5 bet

11.2
A 1 could have called 2 should 3 might
   4 shouldn't 5 might 6 shouldn't
B 1 It shouldn't be difficult to get
   2 You could have told us
   3 He won't get in
   4 we might as well get
   5 You should wear
   6 Kate should have arrived
C 1 won't 2 might 3 shouldn't 4 might
   5 might 6 could
D Students' own answers

11.3
A 1 b 2 d 3 a 4 e
B 1 Over 2 intimate 3 difficult 4 fewer
   5 home
C 1 menacing 2 strike up 3 eligible
   4 screening 5 would-be 6 abode
   7 bail 8 coaxing 9 rolling the dice

11.4
A 1 – 2 The 3 – 4 a 5 – 6 animals
   7 the 8 them 9 people 10 a 11 an
   12 the
B 1 **a** terrible flight 2 correct 3 most of ~~them~~ **it** 4 **a** record number 5 correct
C 1 an, the 2 the, them 3 an, it 4 the, a
D Students' own answers

11.5
A 1 over 65 2 on the stairs and out of windows 3 15 minutes 4 faulty equipment (e.g. heaters) 5 the bedroom
B 1 occur 2 reports 3 are 4 involve
   5 happen 6 are 7 are 8 live 9 are
   10 include
C 1 hives 2 swelling 3 doom 4 cramps
D 1 the word *safe*
   2 the grammar: special uses of modals (*won't* for refusal)
   3 dating and love
   4 the grammar: definite and indefinite articles (pattern b, lightning)
   5 safety (horseback riding)
E Students' own answers

Unit 12
12.1
A 1 e 2 d 3 a 4 f 5 b
B 1 a 2 c 3 c 4 b 5 a 6 b
C 1 stems 2 pave 3 closely 4 rise
D 1 skyrocketed 2 soar 3 plunged
   4 fall 5 leveled off

12.2
A 1 Being interpreted 2 being used
   3 to be seen 4 not be considered
   5 being seen
B 1 looking forward to it being played 2 to be played 3 Being offered 4 couldn't be played 5 difficult to be taken 6 couldn't stand being rejected
C Across: 2 grow on 5 bring about
   Down: 1 fall back on 2 warm up to
   4 catch on 6 get across

D Students' own answers

12.3
A 3
B 1 F 2 T 3 F 4 F 5 T 6 F
C 1 leaps 2 namely 3 prescient 4 wacky
   5 pitfalls 6 random 7 undergoing
   8 farsighted

12.4
A 1 got promoted 2 get fired 3 was having some work done 4 getting hassled
   5 was having my work criticized 6 was broken into 7 got the police involved
   8 had all the stolen items recovered
B 1 ~~have~~ be/get 2 have your house repossessed 3 Correct 4 ~~took~~ taken
   5 get us arrested 6 ~~been~~ being
C 1 c 2 e 3 a 4 d 5 b
D Students' own answers

12.5
A a there has been a steady decline in the number of people who work outside the home
   b there has been a huge increase in the number of people using social media
   c there has been a steady rise in criticisms of its effect on our well being
   d there has been a dramatic increase in the number of "clickbait" articles
   e there has been a steep rise in the number of work opportunities
B 1 b 2 c 3 a 4 e 5 d
C 1 shorter attention spans, jealousy, and making unfair comparisons between ourselves and others.
   2 It allows us to stay connected and can provide work opportunities.
   3 sensationalist titles and unchecked "facts"
D 1 trends and the word *wave*
   2 the grammar: passive forms with gerunds and infinitives (pattern 2 in active form)
   3 the future
   4 the grammar: the passive and causative with *get* (causative passive: *get = have*)
   5 improving the world
E Students' own answers

Phrasal verb list

Phrasal verbs are verbs with two or three words: main verb + particle (either a preposition or an adverb). The definitions given below are some of those introduced in iDentities. For a full list, visit www.richmondidentites.com

Transitive phrasal verbs have a direct object; some are separable, others inseparable

Phrasal verb	Meaning
A	
ask someone **over**	invite someone
B	
block something **out**	prevent from passing through (light, noise)
blow something **out**	extinguish (a candle)
bring something **about**	cause to happen
bring something **out**	introduce a new product
bring someone **up**	raise (a child)
bring something **up**	bring to someone's attention
C	
call someone **in**	ask for someone's presence
call something **off**	cancel
carry something **out**	conduct an experiment / plan
cash in on something	profit
catch up on something	get recent information
charge something **up**	charge with electricity
check someone / something **out**	examine closely
check up on someone	make sure a person is OK
cheer someone **up**	make happier
clear something **up**	clarify
come away with something	learn something useful
come down to something	be the most important point
come down with something	get an illness
come up with something	invent
count on someone / something	depend on
crack down on something	take severe measures
cut something **down**	bring down (a tree); reduce
cut someone **off**	interrupt someone
cut something **off**	remove; stop the supply of
cut something **out**	remove; stop doing an action
D	
do something **over**	do again
draw something **together**	unite
dream something **up**	invent
drop someone / something **off**	take someplace
drop out of something	quit
dwell on something	linger over, think hard about something
E	
end up with something	have an unexpected result
F	
face up to something	accept something unpleasant
fall back on something	use an old idea
fall for someone	feel romantic love
fall for something	be tricked into believing
figure someone / something **out**	understand with thought
fill someone **in**	explain
find something **out**	learn information
follow something **through**	complete
G	
get something **across**	help someone understand
get around to something	finally do something
get away with something	avoid the consequences
get off something	leave (a bus, train, plane)
get on something	board (a bus, train, plane)
get out of something	leave (a car); avoid doing something
get to someone	upset someone

Phrasal verb	Meaning
get to something	reach
get together with someone	meet
give something **back**	return
give something **up**	quit
give up on someone / something	stop hoping for change / trying to make something happen
go along with something	agree
grow out of something	stop doing (over time, as one becomes an adult)
H	
hand something **in**	submit
hand something **out**	distribute
help someone **out**	assist
K	
keep someone or something **away**	cause to stay at a distance
keep something **on**	not remove (clothing / jewelry)
keep someone or something **out**	prevent from entering
keep up with someone	stay in touch
L	
lay someone **off**	fire for economic reasons
lay something **out**	arrange
leave something **on**	not turn off (a light or appliance); not remove (clothing or jewelry)
leave something **out**	not include, omit
let someone **down**	disappoint
let someone **off**	allow to leave (a bus, train); not punish
light something **up**	illuminate
look after someone / something	take care of
look down on someone	think one is better, disparage
look into something	research
look out for someone	watch, protect
look someone / something **up**	try to find
look up to someone	admire, respect
M	
make something **up**	invent
make up for something	do something to apologize
miss out on something	lose the chance
P	
pass something **out**	distribute
pass someone / something **up**	reject, not use
pay someone **back**	repay, return money
pay someone **off**	bribe
pay something **off**	pay a debt
pick someone **up**	give someone a ride
pick something **up**	get / buy; learn something; answer the phone; get a disease
point someone / something **out**	indicate, show
pull something **off**	make something happen
put something **away**	return to its appropriate place
put something **back**	return to its original place
put someone **down**	treat with disrespect
put something **off**	delay
put something **together**	assemble, build
put something **up**	build, erect
put up with someone / something	accept without complaining

117

Phrasal verb list

Phrasal verb	Meaning
R	
run into someone	meet
run out of something	not have enough
run something **by** someone	tell someone something so they can give you their opinion
S	
see something **through**	complete
send something **back**	return
send something **out**	mail
set something **up**	establish; prepare for use
settle on something	choose after consideration
show someone / something **off**	display the best qualities
shut something **off**	stop (a machine, light, supply)
sign someone **up**	register
stand up for someone / something	support
stick with / to someone / something	not quit, persevere
straighten something **up**	make neat
switch something **on**	start, turn on (a machine, light)
T	
take over from someone	take control from someone else
take something **away**	remove
take something **back**	return; accept an item; retract a statement
take something **in**	notice, remember; make a clothing item smaller
take someone **on**	hire
take something **on**	agree to a task
take someone **out**	invite and pay for someone
take something **up**	start a new activity (as a habit)
talk someone **into**	persuade
talk something **over**	discuss
tear something **down**	destroy, demolish
tear something **up**	tear into small pieces
think back on something	remember
think something **over**	consider
think something **up**	invent, think of a new idea
tip someone **off**	give someone a hint or warning
touch something **up**	improve with small changes
try something **on**	put on to see if it fits, is desirable (clothing, shoes)
try something **out**	use an item / do an activity to see if it's desirable
turn something **around**	turn so the front faces the back; cause to get better
turn someone / something **down**	reject
turn something **in**	submit
turn someone / something **into**	change from one type or form to another
turn someone **off**	cause to lose interest, feel negatively
turn something **out**	make, manufacture
U	
use something **up**	use completely, consume
W	
wake someone **up**	cause to stop sleeping
walk out on someone	leave a spouse / child / romantic relationship
warm (up) to something/someone	begin to like something or someone
watch out for someone	protect
wear someone/something **out**	damage from too much use
wipe something **out**	remove, destroy
work something **out**	calculate mathematically; solve a problem
write something **down**	create a written record (on paper)
write something **up**	write in a finished form

Intransitive phrasal verbs
have no direct object; they are all inseparable

A	
act up	behave inappropriately
B	
blow over	pass, be forgotten
break down	stop functioning
break up	end a relationship
C	
catch on	become popular
check in	report arrival (at a hotel, airport)
check out	pay a bill and leave (a hotel)
cheer up	become happier
come along	go with, accompany
come up	arise (an issue)
D	
doze off	fall asleep unintentionally
dress up	wear more formal clothes; a costume
drop in	visit unexpectedly
drop out	quit
E	
eat out	eat in a restaurant
F	
fall through	fail to happen
find out	learn new information
follow through	finish, complete something
G	
get ahead	make progress, succeed
get along	have a good relationship
get by	survive
get through	finish; survive
go along	accompany; agree
go away	leave a place
go on	continue
H	
hang up	end a phone call
hold on	wait (often during a phone call)
K	
keep away	stay at a distance
keep on	continue
keep up	maintain speed / momentum
L	
lie down	recline (on a bed / floor / sofa)
light up	illuminate; look pleased, happy
look out	be careful
M	
make up	end an argument
miss out	lose the chance (for something good)
P	
pass out	become unconscious, faint
pay off	be worthwhile
pick up	improve
pop up	occur unexpectedly
R	
run out	leave suddenly; not have enough (a supply)
S	
show up	appear; arrive at a place
sign up	register
slip up	make a mistake
stay up	not go to bed
T	
take off	leave, depart (a plane); succeed, achieve success
turn in	go to sleep
turn out	have a certain result
turn up	appear
W	
wear off	disappear, diminish slowly

Richmond

58 St Aldates
Oxford
OX1 1ST
United Kingdom

ISBN: 978-84-668-2801-7
DL: M-23088-2017
First Edition: July 2017
© Richmond / Santillana Global S.L.

All rights reserved. No part of this book may be reproduced, stored in a retrieval system or transmitted in any form by any means, electronic, mechanical, photocopying, recording or otherwise, without the prior permission in writing of the Publisher.

Richmond publications may contain links to third party websites. We have no control over the content of these websites, which may change frequently, and we are not responsible for the content or the way it may be used with our materials. Teachers and students are advised to exercise discretion when accessing links.

Publishing Director: Deborah Tricker

Editors: Deborah Goldblatt, Laura Miranda, Shona Rodger

Proofreaders: Tas Cooper, Cathy Heritage, Fiona Hunt, Kate Mellersh, Tania Pattison, Sophie Sherlock

Project and Cover Design: Lorna Heaslip

Layout: Oliver Hutton (H D Design), Dave Kuzmicki

Picture Researcher: Magdalena Mayo, Arnos Design Ltd

Illustrators: Aviel Basil, Ricardo Bessa, John Holcroft, Oivind Hovland, Andres Lozano, lynton@kja-artists, sean@kja-artists, Pablo Velarde

Digital Content: Luke Baxter, Anup Dave

Audio Recording: Motivation Sound Studios

Texts:

p. 32 https://www.mindtools.com/CommSkll/PublicSpeaking.htm
© Mind Tools Ltd, 1996-2016. All rights reserved. "Mind Tools" is a registered trademark of Mind Tools Ltd. Reproduced with permission.

p. 43 http://www.scientificamerican.com/article/why-do-some-people-believe-in-conspiracy-theories/
Reproduced with permission. Copyright © 2016, Scientific American, a division of Nature America, Inc. All rights reserved.

p. 64 *The Way Up to Heaven* extract (first published in *The New Yorker*, 1954). Published in Penguin Books in the collection *Kiss Kiss*, a collection of short stories. Copyright © Roald Dahl Nominee Ltd, 1954. Reproduced with permission.
Illustration for *The Way Up To Heaven* copyright © Eleanor Percival

p. 76 http://listverse.com/2016/01/24/10-things-you-didnt-know-babies-could-do/
Reproduced with permission.

p. 86 http://www.fastcompany.com/3012939/the-true-story-of-amazing-customer-service-from-gasp-an-airline
Used with permission of Fast Company Copyright© 2016. All rights reserved.

p. 98 http://www.huffingtonpost.com/kerri-zane/5-reasons-its-better-to-b_b_2854313.html
Reproduced with permission.

p. 108 https://www.psychologytoday.com/blog/looking-in-the-cultural-mirror/201009/are-american-friendships-superficial
Reproduced with permission of Jefferson M. Fish Copyright© 2016. All rights reserved.

p. 120 http://www.aarp.org/home-family/dating/info-01-2013/online-dating-safety-tips-solin.html
Reprinted from January 9, 2013 AARP.org. Copyright © 2013. All rights reserved.

p. 130 http://www.wired.com/2014/05/victorian-postcards-predict-future/
Reproduced with permission Copyright © 2016 Condé Nast. All rights reserved.

Photos:
500PX MARKETPLACE/Brian Bonham; ALAMY/Kaleidoscope, Steve Stock, BSIP SA, Cultura RM, MBI, Home People, Rob Walls, Alex Segre, Image Source, David Cole, age fotostock, Peter Forsberg, Maurice Savage, RayArt Graphics, CBW, Stock Photo, blickwinkel, Blend Images, AF archive, Richard Levine, Vadym Drobot, Jack Sullivan, SilverScreen, Ian Allenden, Web Pix, Eden Breitz, David Levenson, Ferne Arfin, Ed Rooney, Xinhua, Mike Kiev, Roberto Herrett, Lynne Sutherland, ZUMA Press, Inc., Eric D ricochet69, Nicholas Stratford, Wavebreak Media ltd, World History Archive, Stacy Walsh Rosenstock, epa european pressphoto agency b.v., Clare Gainey; ARNOS DESIGN LTD./David Oakley; CARTOONSTOCK/Eldon Pletcher, Aaron Bacall, Fran; GETTY IMAGES SALES SPAIN/Howard Kingsnorth, HeroImagesCLOSED, Francisco Romero, Eyecandy Images, Hero Images, Thinkstock; GLASBERGEN CARTOON SERVICE/Randy Glasbergen/www.glasbergen.com; ISTOCKPHOTO/Getty Images Sales Spain; OFF THE MARK CARTOONS/Mark Parisi; PBS/PBS Newshour; REX SHUTTERSTOCK/Ricardo Demurez / imageBROKER, Everett Collection, Blend Images, Broadimage, WestEnd61, SNAP; SHUTTERSTOCK NETHERLANDS,B.V.; WATCHMOJO/ www.watchmojo.com; ZUMA PRESS/Bryan Smith; Dr. Cialdini/ www.influenceatwork.com; Eleanor Percival; Chic by CHoice; Alinea Egmont; ARCHIVO SANTILLANA; Kirby Lee - USA TODAY Sports; ALAMY/ Andres Rodriguez, PhotoAlto, Loop Images Ltd.; GETTY IMAGES SALES SPAIN/Kim Kulish, Carolyn Cole, Stokbyte, Paul Drinkwater/NBCU Photo Bank, David Freund; ISTOCKPHOTO/Getty Images Sales Spain; ROALD DAHL NOMINEE LTD; SHUTTERSTOCK NETHERLANDS,B.V.; Andrew Smith; ARCHIVO SANTILLANA

The Publisher has made every effort to trace the owner of copyright material; however, the Publisher will correct any involuntary omission at the earliest opportunity.

Printed in Brazil by Forma Certa Gráfica Digital, 2024
Lote: 788062